[A~~SSHOLES~~]

Also by Aaron James

Fairness in Practice: A Social Contract
for a Global Economy

[ASSHOLES]

A Theory

Aaron James

NICHOLAS BREALEY
PUBLISHING
London • Boston

This paperback edition first published in the UK by
Nicholas Brealey Publishing in 2013

3–5 Spafield Street
Clerkenwell, London
EC1R 4QB
Tel: +44 (0)20 7239 0360
Fax: +44 (0)20 7239 0370

20 Park Plaza
Boston
MA 02110, USA
Tel: 888 BREALEY
Fax: (617) 523 3708

www.nicholasbrealey.com

ISBN: 978-1-85788-610-8
eISBN: 978-1-85788-956-7

British Library Cataloguing in Publication Data
A catalogue record for this book is available from the British Library.

Book design by Michael Collica
Jacket design by Emily Mahon

Printed in the UK by Clays Ltd, St Ives plc.

To my parents

If an individual takes a lenient view of the moral law, he may well have a high opinion of himself and be conceited, because he judges himself by a false standard.

—IMMANUEL KANT, *Lectures on Ethics*

Émile, in considering his rank in the human species and seeing himself so happily placed there, will be tempted to . . . attribute his happiness to his own merit. . . . This is the error most to be feared, because it is the most difficult to destroy.

—JEAN-JACQUES ROUSSEAU, *Émile*

Do you know who I am?

—A quintessential asshole question

CONTENTS

[ASSHOLES]

[1] A THEORY

In the summer of 2010, Stanley McChrystal, U.S. army general and Afghan war commander, reportedly trashed the U.S. civilian military leadership, in effect forcing President Barack Obama to ask him to resign. The display of disrespect was striking, and it can easily seem to tell against McChrystal's character, especially if reports are true about his handling of smaller matters. According to one story, McChrystal was once apprised by his chief of staff that he was obliged to attend a dinner in Paris with NATO allies—if not to shore up flagging support for the war, then simply because, as the chief of staff put it, "the dinner comes with the position, sir." McChrystal apparently held up his middle finger, retorting, "Does this come with the position?"[1]

For brazen disregard, General McChrystal pales in comparison to another general, Douglas MacArthur. During the Korean War, MacArthur was a law unto himself, in matters both big and small. He quarreled defiantly in public with President Truman, agitating for nuclear war. In their eventual confrontation at Wake Island, MacArthur went so far as to arrive first and then order the president's approaching plane into a holding pattern. MacArthur's commander in chief would thus arrive on the landing strip appearing to be MacArthur's supplicant.

---

1. Michael Hastings, "The Runaway General," *Rolling Stone,* July 8–22, 2010, www.rollingstone.com/politics/news/17390/119236.

In explaining why he subsequently relieved MacArthur of his command, Truman said, "I fired him because he wouldn't respect the authority of the president. I didn't fire him because he was a dumb son of a bitch, although he was, but that's not against the law for generals."[2] Truman was arguably pulling his punches. He could easily have called MacArthur an asshole.

That would not be an exotic charge: assholes abound in history and public life. Aside from runaway generals, we might think of such contemporary figures as former Italian president Silvio Berlusconi, Venezuelan president Hugo Chavez, or Iranian president Mahmoud Ahmadinejad. We might think of the self-important developer-entertainer Donald Trump, the harsh pop music critic Simon Cowell, or the narcissist actor Mel Gibson.[3] Assholes are found daily on cable news, where hosts repeatedly interrupt their guests, and also on talk radio, where airtime is given to commentators who thrive on falsehood and invective. Even as this demonstrably degrades the public debate so vital for a healthy democratic society, overheated commentators get rich and famous, while clearly having a really great time.

All of this poses a larger philosophical question: What is it for someone to be an asshole? The answer is not obvious, despite the fact that we are often personally stuck dealing with people for whom there is no better name. Assholes can be found not simply in history and high public office but almost anywhere—at work; in our chosen club, sport, school, religious

2. Merle Miller, *Plain Speaking: An Oral Biography of Harry S. Truman* (New York: Berkley, 1974).
3. David Brooks all but calls Gibson an asshole in "The Gospel of Mel Gibson," *New York Times,* July 15, 2010, www.nytimes.com/2010/07/16/opinion/16brooks.html.

group, or circle of friends; and even, for the truly unlucky, in the home or immediate family. Try as we might to avoid them, we often simply have to manage encounters that come, for most of us, with great difficulty and personal strain. The asshole is not just another annoying person but a deeply bothersome person—bothersome enough to trigger feelings of powerlessness, fear, or rage. To make matters worse, we may be unable to understand why exactly someone should be so disturbing. We may feel certain only that "asshole" is a suitably unsavory name for this particular person.

While most of us could use advice in asshole management, we cannot get far without an answer to our initial question: What is it for someone to be an asshole?[4] If nothing else, a good answer—a good theory of the asshole—would be intellectually interesting. It would give us the concepts to finally think or say why some people disturb us so. That, in turn, would ideally open a window into deeper aspects of morality and social life. We would see what assholes reveal about the human social condition and why assholes are everywhere, in every society. Ideally, a good theory would be practically useful. Understanding the asshole we are stuck with might help us think constructively about how best to handle him. We might get a better sense of when the asshole is best resisted and when he is best ignored—a better sense of what is, and what is not, worth fighting for.

4. Robert I. Sutton, *The No Asshole Rule: Building a Civilized Workplace and Surviving One That Isn't,* 1st ed. (New York: Warner Business Books, 2007), advises business managers to adopt a policy of zero tolerance of assholes in the workplace, offering helpful suggestions about how to deal with them when they simply cannot be fired. Our initial target is a philosophical account that might support and supplement the good advice already available.

According to our theory, which we will present shortly, the asshole exposes a deep feature of morality that philosophers have sought to understand from the time of Jean-Jacques Rousseau to this day.[5] The asshole refuses to listen to our legitimate complaints, and so he poses a challenge to the idea that we are each to be recognized as moral equals. This explains why the asshole is so bothersome, by revealing the great importance we attach to recognition in unexpected areas of our lives. In later chapters, we will suggest that a clearer understanding of this helps with asshole management. The key is to understand why we are easily tempted to fight on the asshole's terms: we are fighting for moral recognition in his eyes. We will also explore larger, more basic questions about human social life. Why are assholes mainly men? Can assholes be properly blamed? Why do some societies produce more assholes than others? Are certain styles of capitalism especially prone to asshole production and thus social decline? And, finally, can we ultimately make peace not only with the given asshole but also with a human social condition in which assholes flourish?

WHAT IS IT TO BE AN ASSHOLE?

Our theory is simply this: a person counts as an *asshole* when, and only when, he systematically allows himself to enjoy special advantages in interpersonal relations out of an entrenched

---

5. Our hero Rousseau was unfortunately quite an asshole himself, or maybe something worse. He eventually realized that something was amiss in his repeatedly fathering children with Thérèse Lavasseur and then summarily sending them away to an orphanage. See *The Confessions of Jean-Jacques Rousseau*, trans. J. M. Cohen (London: Penguin, 1953).

sense of entitlement that immunizes him against the complaints of other people. (Because assholes are by and large men, we use the masculine pronoun "he" advisedly. We will suggest that women can be assholes as well. For the time being, think of Ann Coulter. We consider the question of gender in detail in chapter 4.) Our theory thus has three main parts. In interpersonal or cooperative relations,[6] the asshole:

(1) allows himself to enjoy special advantages and does so systematically;

(2) does this out of an entrenched sense of entitlement; and

(3) is immunized by his sense of entitlement against the complaints of other people.

So, for example, the asshole is the person who habitually cuts in line. Or who frequently interrupts in a conversation. Or who weaves in and out of lanes in traffic. Or who persistently emphasizes another person's faults. Or who is extremely sensitive to perceived slights while being oblivious to his crassness with others. An insensitive person—a mere "jerk"—might allow himself to so enjoy "special advantages" in such interpersonal relations. What distinguishes the asshole is the *way* he acts, the reasons that motivate him to act in an abusive and arrogant way. The ass-

6. By "interpersonal" relations we mean cooperative relations with a more or less socially defined structure, in contrast, say, with individuals interacting in a condition of anarchy such as Thomas Hobbes's famous state of nature. If one can be an asshole in the state of nature, Hobbes would regard this as fully justified self-defense. In conditions of society, by contrast, assholes are akin to Hobbes's famous Foole, who joins the social contract but then breaks or cheats the law.

hole acts out of a firm sense that *he is special*, that the normal rules of conduct do not apply to him. He may not deliberately exploit interpersonal relations but simply remains willfully oblivious to normal expectations. Because the asshole sets himself apart from others, he feels entirely comfortable flouting accepted social conventions, almost as a way of life. Most important, he lives this way more or less out in the open. He stands unmoved when people indignantly glare or complain. He is "immunized" against anyone who speaks up, being quite confident that he has little need to respond to questions about whether the advantages he allows himself are acceptable and fair. Indeed, he will often *himself* feel indignant when questions about his conduct are raised. That, from his point of view, may show that he is not getting the respect he deserves.

Although our theory is a definition of the term "asshole," we should emphasize that it is not necessarily a dictionary definition. It is not necessarily a claim about how the word "asshole" is commonly used in some linguistic group (e.g., speakers of English). The word is often used loosely and variously, and we aren't suggesting that every competent speaker of English would agree with our proposal about what the word means. We aren't even saying that a majority of speakers would agree, in a way that might be confirmed or undermined by opinion polls or psychological experiments. Instead, our approach is the one Socrates proposes to Polus in Plato's *Gorgias,* when he explains why the dispute between them does not depend on opinion polls (what they call "the company"). Polus asks, "But do you not think, Socrates, that you have been sufficiently refuted, when you say that which no human being will allow? Ask the company." Socrates replies:

> You must not ask me to count the suffrages of the company [. . . .] I shall produce one witness only of the truth of my words, and he is the person with whom I am arguing; his suffrage I know how to take; but with the many I have nothing to do, and do not even address myself to them. May I ask then whether you will answer in turn and have your words put to the proof?[7]

Our definition, in other words, is a *constructive proposal*. It tries to articulate what we ordinarily mean when we speak of "assholes" but ultimately stands or falls on whether it captures the importance assholes have for us—where the "us" is, in the first instance, you and me. I am proposing the definition in light of importance that assholes have for us. You decide whether you agree.[8]

THE PUZZLE

Before considering the details of our theory, we will first follow philosophical practice and ask what kind of theory we are looking for. We can then "test" a given theory—including the one just stated—by considering whether it explains what we are trying to explain. This gives us a modicum of control in a messy enterprise.

We begin with a puzzle. Although some assholes take a staggering toll on the lives of others, many assholes are not bad

7. Translation by Benjamin Jowett, http://classics.mit.edu/Plato/gorgias.html.
8. The point carries over to other proposals in moral theory. "Experimental philosophy" isn't fit to establish or refute them, at least not without further, properly controversial assumptions about what a given proposal is trying to do.

in this way: the costs they impose upon other people may be moderate or small. Yet they are still clearly morally reprehensible. How could that be? Why would we be deeply bothered even by a person who makes little material difference to our lives?

In other words, we might put the puzzle this way. There are at least three things we should want from a good theory of assholes, but it is not immediately obvious how all three might be true.

The first is straightforward: we are looking for a stable trait of character, or type of person—a *vice* rather than a particular act, mere lapse in conduct, or brief phase of life. A single courageous or magnanimous act does not make for a courageous or magnanimous person. Nor does an occasional impatient or self-absorbed or foolish act make someone into an impatient or self-absorbed or foolish person. In the same way, someone can *act like* an asshole—in a particular situation or over a particular day or week—without really, ultimately, *being* an asshole.[9] When the assholish behavior doesn't reflect the kind of person someone generally is, stably, in his life, he is better classified as a *jerk,* a *boor,* a *cad,* a *schmuck,* or a mere *ass.* What we want to understand, in the first instance, is the sort of person for whom assholish acts are quite *in* character, and indeed routine, because they *do* generally reflect the type of person he stably is. In particular, our target is the *average proper asshole.* We first seek neither the "royal asshole," who is distinguished even among assholes, nor the "borderline asshole," whose sta-

9. This is probably true of McChrystal, who not only apologized for the disdainful comments mentioned earlier but also has a long track record of dedicated public service.

tus as an asshole is not entirely clear. We want to identify the mean asshole between these extremes: your normal, everyday asshole.

This also means that we should not think first of extreme cases such as Hitler, Stalin, or Mussolini. There are not enough harsh names for these figures, and it is fine to add "asshole" to the list. But it would be deeply offensive to *only* call Hitler or Stalin an asshole; there are much more important ways to describe them morally. At least initially, the *mere* asshole is a less confusing test case.

It should be said that we do not mean to prematurely close the possibility that talk of "assholes" really isn't about any stable trait of character at all but is merely a form of swearing or term of abuse.[10] We certainly do swear at people and use this term, as when one says, "You disgust me, asshole!" Many more clearly descriptive terms ("coward" or "bully," for example) lack the same special expressive power. But the term "asshole" can be expressive and *also* pick out a real feature of persons. It would not be incoherent to say of someone, without disapproval, "He is my friend, and he is fine to me personally, but I have to admit he is an asshole." One might wonder why someone who said this stays friends with an asshole, but the statement could be

10. Harry G. Frankfurt, in *On Bullshit* (Princeton, NJ: Princeton University Press, 2005), plausibly shows how the term "bullshit" has rich descriptive content, even as it initially appears as a term of abuse. The same may be true of "chickenshit" and "horseshit," which differ from each other and from "bullshit" in descriptive meaning. Our inquiry lies within this distinguished line of research. We hope our theory prompts one to think, "Hey, I've met that guy," and thus provides demonstrative evidence that there is at least one asshole and probably more. One could so embrace the existence of assholes even if one had quibbles about the theory's details.

quite *true* and known to all: the person spoken of is, in fact, an asshole.[11]

The second and third things a theory of assholes should explain are related and must be handled with greater care. The second thing to explain is that most assholes are *not* morally beyond the pale, unlike, say, a murderer, rapist, or tyrant. Most assholes are not *that* bad. One post in the Urban Dictionary has it that "[an asshole is] the worst kind of person. . . . If you're an asshole, you are disgusting, loathsome, vile, distasteful, wrathful, belligerent, agoraphobic, and more. . . . [Assholes] are the lowest of the low. They transcend all forms of immorality."[12]

---

11. Someone actually spoke (roughly) the stated sentence to me spontaneously in conversation. That isn't decisive evidence that it can be *true or false* to say that someone is an asshole, and not simply a way of expressing one's feelings of disapproval (as in saying "boo!" to the opposing sports team or in using harsh terms such as "shithead" or "cocksucker," which invoke an unflattering descriptive image without making any claim to truth, properly speaking). Further evidence would be a conditional sentence such as "If an asshole cuts you off in traffic, then it is appropriate to lay on the horn." Here the term "asshole" does not plainly reflect either approval or disapproval. Still better evidence is a sentence that expresses *thoroughgoing endorsement,* such as "Yes, I am an asshole, and proud of it," perhaps said in all sincerity by a supreme asshole who is taunting his subjects with this pronouncement. See *The Onion*'s headline "Asshole Admits to Being Asshole in Supreme Asshole Move," May 19, 2004, www.theonion.com/articles/asshole-admits-to-being-asshole-in-supreme -asshole,1172/. We can add that taking asshole discourse to aim at stating truths doesn't mean that we do not *also* use it to swear and express disapproval, as in "Gosh, *what* an asshole!" or "That guy is *such* an asshole!" When a speaker calls someone an asshole, this can be seen to *pragmatically indicate* that he or she disapproves. For this view of moral judgment, see David Copp, "Realist-Expressivism: A Neglected Option for Moral Realism," *Social Philosophy and Policy* 18, no. 2 (2001): 1–43; and Stephen Finlay, "Value and Implicature," *Philosophers' Imprint* 5, no. 4 (July 2005): 1–20, http://hdl.handle.net/ 2027/spo.3521354.0005.004.

12. Eric Melech, www.urbandictionary.com/define.php?term=asshole.

This is overwrought and unhelpful. We can agree that the worst kinds of people can *also* be assholes, but it is not helpful to think first of people at the bottom of the moral barrel—the Hitlers, Stalins, or Mussolinis—since their corruption is wildly over-determined. As suggested earlier, the mere asshole is a clearer target of inquiry and, in any case, often not among the lowest of the low. We are quite justified in removing a murderer or a rapist or a tyrant from society by force, in handcuffs and at the point of a gun; the material costs such people impose upon others are enormous and often beyond repair. But the material costs many assholes impose upon others—a longer wait in line, a snide remark, a ruined afternoon—are often by comparison moderate or very small. It would be indefensible to forcibly remove them from society. Which is of course why we are often stuck inter-acting with them, why they seem to be everywhere.

And yet—and this is the third thing we need to explain—assholes are still repugnant people. Despite the fact that the material costs they impose are often moderate or small, ass-holes are rightly upsetting, even morally outrageous. Something else is deeply bothersome about them, something beyond mere material costs: something bad enough to drive an otherwise coolheaded person into a fit of rage;[13] something that lingers in one's memory like a foul stench; something that warrants a name we use for a part of the body we hide in public, a part of the body that many people feel alienated from and perhaps wish

13. One entry in the Urban Dictionary describes the asshole as "a man who could tempt the Pope into a fight" (Bwillis, www.urbandictionary.com/define .php?term=asshole&page=4). It is apparently true across cultures that the most common source of homicide is "altercations of relatively trivial origin" that often have to do with small slights. See Martin Daly and Margo Wilson, *Homicide* (New Brunswick, NJ: Transaction Publishers, 1988), 125.

wasn't there.[14] It is this bothersome "something" that we want to expose.

To summarize, then, our three requirements for a good theory of assholes are as follows. We are looking for (1) a stable trait of character, (2) that leads a person to impose only small or moderate material costs upon others, (3) but that nevertheless qualifies the person as morally repugnant.

Yet how could a person who imposes only small or modest costs upon others nevertheless count as morally reprehensible? What way of being could possibly be like that? This is not exactly a paradox. It is an interesting puzzle.

THE MORAL ASSHOLE

Recall our theory: a person counts as an *asshole* just in case he systematically allows himself to enjoy special advantages in interpersonal relations out of an entrenched sense of entitlement that immunizes him against the complaints of other people. This theory answers our challenge by zeroing in on a particular, distinctive way of being morally reprehensible. We can bring this out by considering the way our theory is *moral* through and through.

We should pause, however, to worry about overmoralizing. When the writer David Foster Wallace calls John Updike's character Ben Turnbull an asshole (with the clear implication

14. Here I point to a common feeling without denying that many people have a quite different attitude in light of special intimate or recreational purposes. For the general ambivalent or hostile feelings about such matters, see Leo Bersani, "Is the Rectum a Grave?," in *Is the Rectum a Grave?: and Other Essays* (Chicago: University of Chicago Press, 2010).

that Updike is an asshole as well), the main ground for this is Turnbull's (and Updike's) general self-absorption, not his moral faults.[15] We will agree that self-absorption is crucial. We will also admit that there are more general uses of the term "asshole," which we discuss later on. We start with the central, moral case.

According to our theory, the asshole does what he does out of a "sense of entitlement," a sense of what he *deserves,* or is *due,* or has a *right* to. However misguided, the asshole is *morally motivated.* He is fundamentally different from the psychopath, who either lacks or fails to engage moral concepts, and who sees people as so many objects in the world to be manipulated at will. The asshole takes himself to be *justified* in enjoying special advantages from cooperative relations. Given his sense of his special standing, he claims advantages that he thinks no one can reasonably deny him. He is *resentful* or *indignant* when he feels his rights are not respected, in much the same way a fully sociable, cooperative person is.

Assholes and fully cooperative people simply have very different moral views of what their respective entitlements are. To bring out the difference, compare the point of view of "fully cooperative" people. Fully cooperative people, we may say, *see themselves as equals, as having grounds for special treatment only in special circumstances that others will equally enjoy at the appropriate times.* Here are several examples.

15. David Foster Wallace, "Certainly the End of *Something* or Other, One Would Sort of Have to Think (Re John Updike's *Toward the End of Time*)," in *Consider the Lobster* (New York: Little, Brown, 2006). Originally published as "John Updike, Champion Literary Phallocrat, Drops One; Is This Finally the End for Magnificent Narcissists?," *New York Observer,* October 13, 1997, www .observer.com/1997/10/john-updike-champion-literary-phallocrat-drops-one -is-this-finally-the-end-for-magnificent-narcissists/.

On one's birthday, one expects to receive special indulgences from one's friends, such as a party, a round of drinks, or a celebratory phone call. Yet all count as equals because everyone is assigned one such day of celebration each year on or around the calendar day of each person's birth. If you are celebrating my existence now, I will be celebrating your existence at some point during the year.

The practice of forming a queue will degenerate into a scrum unless people by and large are willing to wait in the line. Yet it would be acceptable for you to cut to the front when you explain that there is a real emergency. You then receive a benefit because others accept a certain burden: if they weren't waiting in line, there would be no line for you to cut in, and you might not be to able work your way to the front in a scrum. But under exigent circumstances, people of course understand. They will do likewise when an emergency comes up in their lives.

Two people will have a successful conversation, in which both speak and both are understood, only when each listens while the other talks and each is given a good amount of speaking time. Yet it is fine to interrupt someone speaking in order to make an especially important point, even if one's excitement to make the point simply gets the best of one. We give each other this privilege, and we are happy to work around occasional interventions, as long as we both feel our conversation is moving along just fine.

Being someone's friend requires consistent efforts to think of and present the friend in a good, supportive light. Yet it can be fine to point out a flaw, as gentle teasing or in order to crack a good joke. The joke can come at the friend's expense if its "price" in discomfiture is low—low enough so that the friend is happy to pay for the sake of a laugh.

We might generalize from these examples in the following way. In each case, there are both normal expectations and special circumstances in which those expectations are, for certain parties, to be set aside. Those who happen to wind up in the special circumstances are permitted to take special benefits, advantages, or treatment, but not because they are themselves special. All are seen as, at bottom, equals. Each will have days of special privilege, as the occasion (e.g., birthday) arises in the normal course of things. And as long as we each take special advantages for good reasons of the right kinds—there really is a grave emergency—no one will be terribly bothered about how the exact distribution of benefits and burdens falls out. We say, "It will all work out in the end," not as a *prediction* about the future (when is "the end"?) but as a vote of confidence: if we really are working together in good faith, accommodating one another for what we can each regard as good reasons of the right sorts, that would in and of itself realize a kind of relationship we could really value, quite aside from the outcomes that fate and circumstance ultimately bring.

The asshole, by contrast, sees no need to wait for special circumstances to come his way in the normal course of things. The asshole feels entitled to allow himself special advantages as he pleases systematically, across a wide range of social interactions. He cuts in line, *and* interrupts often, *and* drives without particular care, *and* persistently highlights people's flaws. He rides people with wearing comments—veiled criticisms, insinuating questions, or awkward allusions to topics not normally discussed in polite company. He is often rude or more often borderline nasty. One feels he has just been intrusive or inconsiderate, though one can't always pinpoint the norm of courtesy he has tread upon. Most important, the asshole gains special advantages from interpersonal relations, not by stroke of continuous luck, but because he regards himself as special. His circumstances are special in each case, in his view, because *he* is in them. If one is special on one's birthday, the asshole's birthday comes every day.

None of this is to say that the asshole never shows restraint. Some assholes are indeed scrappy, acting unreflectively on any inclination and whim, though with varying degrees of success. The witty and charming asshole, however, will get away with more than a dull asshole can. A quite different stripe of asshole shows "principled" restraint when the advantages come too easily. Taking every last advantage, without at least a slight challenge, may seem beneath him, even undignified. He may, so he says, have better, perhaps nobler things to do with his precious time. The "dignified asshole" will share our displeasure with the scrappy asshole and may even hold a special contempt for his lax and unprincipled ways. Yet the dignified asshole is not so "principled" as to forgo the systematic enjoyment of special advantages; he may simply be especially good at justifying the special advantages he takes in his own eyes, by concocting "principled" rationalizations on the fly.

To elaborate on a specific example, consider asshole surfers. Surfers usually have to share relatively few waves and generally do so according to rules of right-of-way that are well understood and more or less the same worldwide. When one surfer is "in position" on the most critical part of a wave, for example, other surfers are expected to yield. Lance the surfer, however, has decided that he should have almost any wave he wants. According to Lance, when people see him paddling for a wave, they should realize that he is the regular, that he's the better—or at least older—surfer, and that this wave is therefore his wave.

It is his wave, even if someone is already in position or up and surfing. Lance lumbers to his feet and surfs anyway, as though he is riding the wave alone. When surfers are "burned" in this way, most complain; they say some version of "Hey, man, what the fuck." When people complain to Lance, he launches into a tirade. "Don't you dare fucking fuck with me!" If the surfer replies, Lance escalates. "If you want some of this, let's take it to the beach! Get the fock out of here! Before I get angry." (If this does not seem plausible, be reassured that Lance can be found in surfing areas worldwide. The police tend not to get involved until violence breaks out.)

Or consider a quite different area of life, academia. Dominic, a historian, has written some rightly acclaimed books. Having become accustomed to feeling appreciated, he now feels entitled to recognition and is especially prone to feeling slighted when he is not given a lot of attention. He finds it outrageous when his work is not cited, or when he is invited to speak at a conference but not offered the keynote address. None of this leads him to doubt whether his work is of continued importance; he instead concludes that those involved clearly lack judgment. As his prominence declines, instead of becoming increasingly uncertain about his claim to attention, he becomes increasingly concerned about the deteriorating state of his profession. In order to uphold high standards, especially as exemplified in his own work, he regularly writes scathing reviews of recent books, finding little good in them, sparing few terms of abuse, while offering slight evidence of his sweeping criticisms. When books he has trashed become prominent and influential, Dominic takes this as further evidence of falling professional standards.

Assholes therefore come in quite different styles. In order to account for this, we stipulate that there are many ways of *coming to be an asshole,* by coming into the appropriate "sense of entitlement." What is crucial is that the sense of entitlement tells the asshole *that* he deserves, or is due, or has a right to special advantages. The reasons *why* he feels he deserves special treatment may be as diverse as the stars. He may be sure that he is the greatest historian, architect, actor, artist, corporate executive, or political leader seen in a long time. He may feel entitled to his position of power and the control over people it enables him to exercise. When people suffer at his hand, this is simply an unfortunate fact of life—for them. He may feel that the nobility of his character, or the worthiness of his favored social cause, gives him legitimate claim to have things go his way, especially when those who present obstacles can be seen as weak, unworthy, or morally corrupt. He may find most people tediously unintelligent or dull, in contrast with his own brilliant mind and manner. He may relate to them as though doing a chore, and even congratulate himself on his heroic success in treating such unworthy people politely. These are all different ways of having the appropriate "sense of entitlement." If we had a taxonomy of such different entitlement conceptions, we would have a taxonomy of the different species of asshole. (We make a start on that effort in chapters 2 and 3.)

We should emphasize that one is not an asshole simply for taking oneself to be entitled to certain things. Under the appropriate circumstances, we all have a right to be told the truth, not to be kicked or cheated, or even to receive certain special advantages from cooperative life. And one is not an asshole simply for being mistaken about what one's entitlements are. We all make such mistakes from time to time. What makes someone an asshole is a special way of being wrong about what one's entitlements are: the asshole's "entrenched sense of entitlement" leads him to systematically think or assume that he has special entitlements that, from a moral point of view, he does not have. Again, that distinctive kind of error may come in very different forms. The asshole might invoke a genuine entitlement principle but misapply it to his particular situation. Or he might easily find entitlement rationalizations on the fly for whatever he happens to want at the time. In either case, the crucial feature is that the asshole's entrenched sense of entitlement produces some such form of moral error in a systematic way. It is in that general way that the asshole treats himself as morally special.

Of course, we often disagree about what entitlements people do or do not have, especially in political life. That means we will often disagree about who is or is not an asshole. For example, according to Lefty, Bill O'Reilly is an asshole. He is opportunistically exploiting working-class resentment. And according to Righty, O'Reilly is no asshole. He is heroically giving voice to working-class resentment. According to our theory, whether O'Reilly counts as an asshole depends on whether *he is in fact entitled* to act as he acts. People can disagree about that, given their background views about his social role and its value or disvalue, without disagreeing about what it is to be an asshole generally. So both Lefty and Righty can accept our theory. Lefty can say that O'Reilly is an asshole but happily admit that this wouldn't be so if Righty were correct that O'Reilly is entitled to do as he does (and vice versa). The same is true of the many examples discussed in chapters 2 and 3. Many won't agree with the moral diagnoses I offer of those figures. Even so, we can all agree about what the essence of the asshole is.

TAKING STOCK

Let us return to the three things we said that any good theory
of assholes should explain and take stock of how our theory
explains each of them.

The first is relatively straightforward: we are looking for a
stable trait of character. Our theory picks out a stable trait
of character because the asshole's sense of entitlement is
"entrenched" in his motivational makeup: the feeling of entitlement does not merely occasionally spring up, like a sudden urge
to watch a B movie. Nor is the feeling reoccurring but readily
struck down. A person of good conscience might be aware of
his own inner asshole and yet often successfully remind himself that his life is of no more importance than anyone else's,
that his own talents and accomplishments are largely a matter of luck, and that he is fortunate to live well and savor the
sweetness of people in normal cooperative life. The asshole
not only lacks such motivational correctives, his sense of entitlement is "entrenched," in the sense that he is persistently
assured, even upon reflection, that he is quite unlike everyone else. When the world questions his special standing in it,
it is the challenge rather than the standing that gives way.
The asshole sees no need to defend his special place in the
social world, or he easily produces convincing rationalizations and moves on. He may even compliment himself on his
resiliency and formidable argumentative powers. If reflection
is for most people an important source of moral learning, the
asshole puts reflection mainly in the service of assuring himself. This leaves him quite impervious to reform. Even when
profound hardships befall him, and there is abundant thera-

peutic help, he will, in all likelihood, never see reason to change.[16]

Let's turn to the second feature to be explained—that the asshole is not invariably bad in terms of the material costs he imposes upon others. We explain this by defining the "special advantages" the asshole takes in a restricted way. There is nothing wrong *in itself* with enjoying the benefit of cutting to the front of a line, or of speaking out of turn, or of being freed from certain responsibilities. These actions are not, as such, wrong in the way it is wrong, say, to kill someone for the sake of fast cash. In general, the goods the asshole allows himself to enjoy flow from social practices that are generally beneficial. We ourselves admit that the asshole, too, should share in those sorts of goods, in the right measure and at the right times. The general problem is that the asshole helps himself to more than his share, or acts out of turn, or sloughs off the burdens that must generally be carried if the practices in question are to work. He can do that without doing irreparable harm or committing clear-cut wrongs. One can be a full-fledged asshole in the small.

This suggests that the asshole is not in any real sense an outlaw. He may well keep within the letter of the law. Nor is he just another cheater, out for a "free ride" on the cooperative efforts of others. The deeper problem is not deliberate exploitation but

16. Many assholes may have what psychologists call "narcissistic personality disorder," which is generally very resistant to therapeutic treatment. As psychologist Sander Koole explained (in conversation), when the therapist asks, "How do you feel?" the narcissist answers, "I feel I am not getting the respect I deserve." While this is characteristic of narcissistic personality disorder, we are not assuming that every such person counts as an asshole. Being an asshole is probably only one version of the disorder. Even so, the near plague of narcissism in our culture might explain why there are more assholes than there used to be. We touch upon this theme at several points later.

a kind of willful insensitivity: he sees no reason to address the ambiguities and uncertainties that inevitably arise when people interact. Even "bright-line" rules of cooperation will have exceptions, and cooperative people often have to put a certain amount of work into discerning both the spirit of the law and what is finally acceptable in a particular case. They thus seek clarification, check assumptions, ask permission, or at least take a measure of care in good faith. The asshole, by contrast, sees little need for the work of mutual restraint aimed at benefit for all involved. According to his generalized sense of entitlement, it is only right and natural that the various advantages of social life should flow his way.

Turn, finally, to our third requirement of explanation: that the asshole is downright upsetting, even outrageous. How could a person who imposes only small or modest costs upon others nevertheless be morally repugnant? Our answer appeals to a crucial aspect of the asshole's entrenched sense of entitlement: it immunizes him against the complaints of other people. The asshole not only takes special privileges but refuses to listen when people complain. When someone says or conveys (as with a glare) something like "The line starts here," "It is not your turn," "What are you trying to say?," or "Could you, please, *let me finish*," the asshole makes no attempt to hear the person out and perhaps delivers a rude retort, such as "Screw you!" He is unwilling to *recognize* anyone who does express a complaint, never considering that the complaint might be legitimate. So although one may only suffer the small material cost of being cut ahead of in line, or being interrupted, or being talked over, one also suffers a deeper wrong: one's very status as a moral person goes unrecognized. Immanuel Kant memorably says that respect for the moral law "strikes down" or "humiliates" our sense of "self-conceit."[17] This doesn't happen for the asshole.

THE IMPORTANCE OF BEING RECOGNIZED

We have suggested that the asshole is morally repugnant because, even when the material costs he imposes are small, he fails to recognize others in a fundamental, morally important way. This is the heart and soul of our account of why the asshole is so bothersome, so we should more fully delve into the moral question—before moving on to less weighty concerns.

Kant would say the asshole suffers from "self-conceit" or "arrogantia." This is supposed to be something different from mere "self-love," which might lead to selfishness but isn't necessarily a corruption of one's capacities to reason morally. One can act selfishly, or even be a selfish person, despite one's better moral judgment, perhaps by ignoring the moral situation or getting oneself not to actively consider it, much as a "jerk" or "schmuck" does. The asshole, by contrast, actively reasons *from* his sense of special entitlement rather than from an independent understanding of what the moral law requires when, in

17. As Kant illustrates, even in encountering "a humble plain man, in whom I perceive righteousness in a higher degree than I am conscious of in myself, *my mind bows* whether I choose or not, however high I carry my head that he may not forget my superior position." Kant is responding to this remark by French popular philosopher Bernard Le Bovier de Fontenelle: "I bow to a great man, but my mind does not bow." "Of the Drives of Pure Practical Reason," in *Critique of Practical Reason,* 3rd ed., ed. and trans. Lewis White Beck (New York: Macmillan, 1993), part 1, book 1, chap. 3, 80. For related discussion, see also *Lectures on Ethics,* trans. Louis Infield with foreword by Lewis White Beck (1963; repr., London: Methuen, 1979), 126–29.

Kant's terms, all are regarded equally as "ends in themselves," as coequal sovereigns in a "Kingdom of Ends."[18]

Here Kant is probably developing Rousseau's distinction between a person's natural sense of self-worth (*amour de soi-même*) and a potentially destructive concern for rank or status as compared to others (*amour propre*).[19] According to Rousseau, healthy self-love does not require comparing oneself to others at all; feeling worthy does not necessarily involve feeling superior to someone. Yet we invariably and rightly do care about how we are regarded by others in our social relationships. If the way of the world is often simply to compete for status, to try to better someone, Rousseau vividly explains how this gives rise to untold personal misery and grave social ills.[20] Even so, nothing in the human social condition per se requires status competition. Instead, Rousseau suggests, we can acknowledge each person's need for status recognition without treating anyone as either better or worse than another; we need only recognize each as fundamentally equal. All can rest content with this solution— except, of course, the asshole. His feelings of *amour propre* are an unquenchable fire. He won't settle for mere equality.[21]

18. Or at least in this one reading of Kant's idea that self-love becomes self-conceit when it "makes itself legislative and the unconditional practical principle" (*Critique of Practical Reason,* p. 77). It also fits with the passage from *Lectures on Ethics* (p. 128) quoted in the epigraph, in which Kant speaks of the conceited person taking a "lenient view of the moral law" and thus having a "false standard." We develop the point further in "Letter to an Asshole."
19. See Jean-Jacques Rousseau, *Émile; or, On Education,* trans. Allan Bloom (New York: Basic Books, 1979).
20. Jean-Jacques Rousseau, "Discourse on the Origins and Foundations of Inequality Among Men," in *A Discourse on Inequality,* trans. Maurice Cranston (New York: Penguin, 1984).
21. In *Émile,* Rousseau speaks of "inflamed *amour propre*" (p. 247) as well as the difficulty of overcoming this mentality (see the passage on p. 245, which is

Other philosophers have developed ideas of "moral status" and "mutual recognition," most notably Fichte (e.g., on how one person's "summons" can awaken another person into freedom and mutual regard), Hegel (on the unequal regard between master and slave), Sartre (on shame or sexual desire), and Buber (on the "I-Thou" relation we stand in to each and all Others, in contrast with the "I-It" relation we bear to mere things). Or as contemporary moral philosophers might say, in blander but perhaps clearer terms, morality is "second personal," in at least the following way.[22]

If being a person with basic moral status means anything, it at the very least means that one is owed respect and consideration as a being endowed with capacity to reason. In particular, people are endowed with powers that enable them to consider and evaluate how someone has acted. A mountain, whale, or tree, though deserving of consideration and appreciation in its own right, lacks the range of abilities needed to question the justifiability of what others have done. The community of persons is, in this way, special.[23] I, as an ordinary human person, have special powers of self-consciousness, reasoning, and judgment. I can observe someone acting, as a mere event in the order of things, but also ask (if only to myself) certain questions

---

quoted in the epigraph). We return to Rousseau's view that destructive status consciousness has a social cause and a political solution in chapter 7.

22. See T. M. Scanlon, *What We Owe to Each Other* (Cambridge, MA: Belknap Press of Harvard University Press, 1998), and especially Stephen Darwall, *The Second-Person Standpoint: Morality, Respect, and Accountability* (Cambridge, MA: Harvard University Press, 2006).

23. But can't one be an asshole for kicking a dog? It seems so, though I'm not sure one would count as an asshole (as opposed to being simply cruel) if one only kicked dogs and treated people perfectly well. But maybe; we can leave the matter open.

of justification. Why, I might ask, should an act such as that be acceptable? In particular, is such an act justifiable to me if it was done in my direction, given how it might affect me?

Likewise, any one of us, so endowed, can ask what would be justifiable to *another* person, from his or her particular point of view. Is that something *she* can reasonably find acceptable, given the consequences for her? Or could she reasonably complain of how she is in effect being treated? In that case, what we think another could or could not accept should have special significance for us and how we act. It will influence our choices, at least if we are at all morally concerned. Each of us, in acting, has to consider not only what might make the world go better rather than worse from an impersonal point of view—factoring in the mountain, the whale, and the tree—but also what could be acceptable *to* each and every other one of us, for reasons arising from the different, distinctive personal standpoint of each separate person in our common world.

That is not to say that just any complaint someone voices in a conversation should carry the day, as though one always needed explicit or implicit permission from everyone who could be affected by one's choices, no matter how unreasonable those people might be. The objections or complaints we actually voice sometimes reflect ignorance of crucial facts or lack of concern with what is reasonably acceptable from everyone's point of view. We can be ignorant or selfish, or both.

Neither are our complaints and objections always or inevitably ill founded in these ways, however. So when someone does object to a particular act, with a quizzical glare or loud words, there is usually *some* reason to think that the person may have a reasonable complaint. Even if the objection is ultimately unreasonable, it also might have an element of truth. Accordingly, one of our basic moral responsibilities is to hear people out, to at least take seriously the reasons they give for wanting to be treated differently, even if we ultimately object. The expectation, in other words, is for us to *recognize* the person objecting, in something like the way a deliberative body grants someone in the room the right to speak before the group. This is, as we might put it, part and parcel of basic *moral respect*—that is, respect not simply for the person's complaint but for the *person* who makes it.

The asshole, by contrast, is wholly *immunized* against the complaints of others. Whether or not the complaint is ultimately reasonable, the person is not registered, from the asshole's point of view, as worthy of consideration. The person who complains is not seen as a potential *source* of reasonable complaint but is simply walled out. If the person complaining is "standing up for herself," in order to be recognized, it is as though she were physically present but morally nonexistent in the asshole's view of the world.

That is why otherwise coolheaded people fall into a fit of rage or lash out at the asshole: they are fighting to be recognized. They are *not* fighting for the small benefit of having the asshole move to the back of the line or, more generally, for a slightly more fair distribution of the benefits and burdens of cooperation. The person taking a stand against the asshole is fighting to be registered in the asshole's point of view as morally real. She struggles not simply to be heard but to be seen. She struggles to be seen, in Thomas Nagel's phrase, as "one among others equally real."[24]

---

24. Thomas Nagel, *The Possibility of Altruism* (1970; repr., Princeton, NJ: Princeton University Press, 1979). Nagel uses this phrase to explain how the ethical egoist, who only sees reason to do what is ultimately in his own interests, fails to see *himself* as but one among equally real others, and so falls into a kind of solipsism. The asshole is not the pure egoist, but otherwise we merely have a different emphasis: the objector seeks to intrude upon the asshole's solipsistic view of the moral world.

The fight can become extraordinarily frustrating because the asshole usually wins: his sense of entitlement is entrenched, so there is usually no getting through. (Hence one may spontaneously desire to give the man a sound beating, as though that would help.)[25] The fully cooperative person is accustomed to listening when people complain, and used to being heard when even a suggestion of complaint is made. That is how cooperative people normally work out what is acceptable to all, what the moral equality of each person requires. This comes to feel natural, expected, a matter of course. The asshole, by contrast, is equally accustomed to walling others out. He does it all the time. This is comfortable for him. And he is exceptionally good at it: when others complain, he easily dismisses the objection, or quickly finds convincing arguments that rationalize the objection away, and moves on. He compliments himself on how good he is at this because he is very good at it indeed.

OVERMORALIZATION?

We have seen that the asshole is important to us for moral reasons. His sense of special entitlement clashes with our own sense that he morally should recognize us as an equal. We have built this sense of entitlement into our basic account of what an asshole *is*. Here, however, one might object that we are overmoralizing the

25. Thus one post to the Urban Dictionary says the asshole is "Someone who seriously needs their ass kicked" (Thomas Huang, www.urbandictionary.com/define.php?term=asshole&page=17). The asshole is interestingly said to *himself need* rough treatment. Perhaps he is better off, on balance, with a few bruises, having come to see the error of his ways. Our suggestion here is not that this is false, but that rough treatment is largely pointless, because it has little to no chance of bringing the asshole around.

asshole concept. Can't someone count as an asshole but wholly lack a sense of moral entitlement? Can't he simply be thoroughly self-absorbed, like Turnbull or Updike, or most teenagers? Can't he simply be extremely difficult or just clueless?

This line of questioning is important because our theory is a proposal about what all assholes have in common. It is a problem if some people fit our definition but do not count as assholes, or if there are true assholes our definition leaves out. Apparent counterexamples such as those just noted could well mean that we should wipe the slate clean and relax our claim that the asshole has a moral sense of entitlement—that we should de-moralize the concept. How, then, might those examples be accounted for?

It is of course fine to *call* someone an asshole when he is simply self-absorbed or extremely difficult to get along with. When someone cuts one off in traffic, one can appropriately call him an asshole without first finding out whether he did this out of entitlement (in asking at the next traffic light, it could become clear that he merely made a mistake). It makes little difference whether the driver really is, strictly speaking, properly classified as an asshole. The same might go for the difficult person. If your friend is flummoxed by his encounters with an especially difficult person, you might say, "Don't worry about it. He's just an asshole," at once affirming your friend's right to better treatment and advising that he probably should not expect the difficult person to change. These ways of calling someone an asshole seem useful and fine, even without looking further into why the person acts as he does.

Yet, even in such cases, it remains an open question whether the person at issue *really is* an asshole, whether he is best

classified as that type of person. Perhaps he is better classified as a jerk, schmuck, or douche bag, or just someone who
is insensitive to social cues. To this classificatory question, our
theory offers an answer: it delineates the class of assholes from
the vast and motley array of personality types. In so defining the
asshole, our strategy is to start by identifying the *significance*
assholes have for us—the significance of moral recognition. We
then tailor our characterization of the person around that kind
of significance. The asshole's entrenched moral sense of entitlement is thus essential for our account. We can happily admit
that there may be marginal or borderline cases that do not quite
fit our theory. But, otherwise, a proper asshole always has an
underlying sense of moral entitlement. We may have to look
deep within his soul to find it, but it is there.

Turnbull's self-absorption might illustrate the point. Wallace
emphasizes it to explain why Turnbull is so unhappy, especially
in light of his "bizarre, adolescent belief that getting to have sex
with whomever one wants whenever one wants to is a cure for
human despair."[26] Wallace naturally also mentions Turnbull's
(and Updike's) misogyny, and indeed the idea of "getting to have
sex with whomever one wants whenever one wants to" can be
seen as a misogynistic entitlement: an unfounded entitlement
to something that, from a moral point of view, must be freely
offered or given, and so won't necessarily be available as one
prefers. Plato or Aristotle would regard a moral vice of character as itself undermining human happiness or flourishing,
which partly just *consists* in virtuous living. But the point might
hold even if we take the more characteristically modern view

26. Wallace, "Certainly the End of *Something* or Other," in *Consider the Lobster,* 59.

that virtue and happiness potentially come apart. Turnbull's unhappy self-absorption can reflect his failure to experience the real and profound connection with others afforded by true mutual respect, a connection that won't necessarily come along with the pleasures of basic consensual physical contact.

We might add that thorough self-absorption is in any case itself a moral failing that indicates entitlement in our sense: the self-absorbed person feels or presumes that he need take no account of others and, if asked, will often give reasons why this is justified ("I can't do it right now," "I'm overwhelmed," "Can't you see that I've got serious problems!"). These are potentially reasons why the person should not be asked to give others what would otherwise be their due, and how we evaluate those reasons will decide whether someone counts as an asshole. If his reasons are good enough (perhaps he is severely depressed), then he is not an asshole. Or even if the reasons given aren't especially good, if he apologizes for his actions later, he isn't an asshole; he is not immunized against the complaints of others in the way the asshole is. Many jerks, schmucks, and clueless or oblivious souls are pretty incorrigible but won't go to bat for that way of being. They might even apologize, even as they easily fall back into their usual ways later that day or week. The asshole is, in contrast, incorrigible in a special, willful, or defensive way.

But what if someone really believes that *everyone* is entitled to look out for number one? He might live in a defensive crouch or posture of selfish opportunism, and perhaps act a lot like an asshole, but he wouldn't say that he's special in any fundamental sense. He'll say that everyone is acting in his same hypercompetitive way and even regret that this is the way of the world. But, so he says, in getting ahead, he's acting within his rights.

Now, if someone really and truly has this cynical view of the world, despite an honest but thwarted desire to cooperate with his fellow moral equals, then he isn't an asshole, even when he acts like one. But if he really is genuine in his views, he'll presumably be open to discuss and reconsider whether his take on the world can be reasonably maintained. He won't then be entrenched and immunized in the asshole's way. On the other hand, many proper assholes *tell themselves* such universalistic stories without believing them deep down. They might even get themselves to *really believe* them mainly to keep themselves reassured. This species of asshole pays homage to morality by invoking a veneer of impartial universality, in contrast with the supremely smug asshole, who needs little more for his for justification beyond saying, "Well, it is *me*. How could *this* [pointing to himself] not deserve special treatment." An asshole can't *simply* take himself as his reason without standing outside morality altogether (making him more like a psychopath).[27] But assholes can vary considerably in the degree to which they require a pretense of universality to keep themselves feeling secure.

27. Nietzsche's Übermensch famously stands beyond conventional morality and prizes the assertion of self above all. As far as I can tell, he can be read in different ways: either as rejecting morality altogether, as endorsing the true universalistic morality of personal authenticity, or as endorsing special privileges for the few who are courageous enough to assert themselves in ways that are in principle available to all. He's closest to the asshole in the latter reading.

❡ Having defined what it is to be an asshole, we now consider who qualifies. Our general definition will not, by itself, name names. It leaves to *us* the delicate job of investigating assholes in their particularity. A theory seeks not to defame but rather to taxonomize—that is, to build a moral typology in the style of Aristotle and the biological sciences he eventually inspired. Given the teeming asshole ecosystem laid before us in history and public life, our task is to identify the best specimens and classify them according to their kinds.

"JUDGE NOT"?

To classify is to judge. Public figures voluntarily submit their candidacy for assholehood to the court of public opinion. Yet we might worry: Is it our place to judge? Does respect for a moral equal, even an asshole equal, require that we "judge not"? In judging that someone is an asshole, do we in effect appoint ourselves to a high court—itself an asshole move?[1]

Not necessarily. If our theory is right, there exists a certain type of moral personality, and it is an objective matter of fact

1. The Supreme Court of Assholedom has been officially chosen; see Matt Taibbi, "The Supreme Court Named," January 31, 2011, www.rollingstone .com/politics/blogs/taibblog/the-supreme-court-named-20110131.

who is or who is not a person of that moral kind. To classify someone as an asshole is not necessarily to swear at him but rather to represent him as the asshole he is, if only for the sake of *understanding* who the assholes are as distinct from everyone else. We needn't even ultimately disapprove. We might take General MacArthur to be an asshole, for example, and yet find the world better, on balance, because of him. Perhaps Japan would not have developed as successfully as it did after World War II had MacArthur not guided the early reconstruction with a sure if heavy hand. Perhaps MacArthur's asshole nature and the deferential Japanese culture were an especially fortunate match. Perhaps, all told, MacArthur was a force for good.

As we classify, we do so provisionally. We happily admit that any examples are properly controversial. To take someone to be an asshole is to make a moral claim about when a person's sense of entitlement exceeds what morality really justifies. Because we often won't agree about when that is so, especially not in public life, there is no separating a particular asshole judgment from a larger moral and political argument about entitlements people have or don't have. I can't make such arguments in a serious way here, so I instead freely offer my own moral opinions, as nothing more than that, mainly for illustrative purposes. Where you disagree with my (left-leaning) political opinions, you might search for a better exemplar of the same general kind.

Public figures are often misrepresented, so naming names poses a risk of unfairness to real people. The public record is itself invariably selective, and we can hardly offer an exhaustive analysis even of what is publicly known. Our aim therefore is not to offer final judgments, but only to tentatively suggest various possible candidates in light of corroborative details. Even seemingly telling details may mislead, however, so to anyone who is misclassified, we apologize ahead of time. As with any taxonomic enterprise, we stand ready to update and revise, in hopes of eventually getting things right. Is it nevertheless an asshole move to *publicly* name names, perhaps by publishing a book about assholes? I hope not. For one thing, it is fair to say that, by publicly misbehaving, the people we name have voluntarily assumed the risk of being called unpleasant names. And in any case, most have already been called an asshole, or an even worse name, and so stand to suffer no further injury merely for being considered a possible asshole in light of evidence already available. Still, if we are unfair, despite our sincere effort to taxonomize with due care, our preemptive apology stands.

So as not to cast the very first stone, we had better start by asking about ourselves: Am I an asshole? Here is one possible test: if you would be willing to call yourself an asshole, this indicates that you are not in fact one. This particular test is flawed; as we have already observed, assholes often shamelessly own the name. Better (but still imperfect) is a test of shame: whether one is at all *worried* by the thought that one counts as an asshole. To the extent that this thought—"An asshole? Me? Really?"—prompts a sense of shame, perhaps with a felt need to take stock and reflect, one probably, to that extent, is not an asshole. (It is fine if you feel a sudden temporary thrill in the idea of transgression or special powers—as one might, for instance, in the thought of bearing Plato's ring of Gyges, which makes its wearer invisible and so able to avoid accountability.[2] If you'd feel shame in the idea of actually going through with

2. See Plato, *The Republic*, book 2.

the transgressions, though, you're probably in the clear.) On the other hand, if the thought of counting as an asshole gives you no pause, if you retort "whatever," or if you feel a stable sense of delight, this is evidence, albeit inconclusive, that you are an asshole. If you feel ambivalent, perhaps wondering whether there is some way to pull off being an asshole, you may be a borderline or half-assed asshole—not quite a proper, full-fledged asshole but nevertheless an important kind of asshole.[3]

We unfortunately lack an equally straightforward test for judging others.[4] There is also less need for one. The fact is that assholes are not especially difficult to spot. The asshole himself will recognize an asshole (and indeed sometimes compete with him for favorable position). But does it take an asshole to know an asshole? No, manifestly not. Of necessity, most people are not assholes, since a critical mass of cooperators is required if there are to be special advantages for the asshole to take. And yet most people have little difficulty singling assholes out.

A careful eye is, however, required in order to discern the subtle differences in asshole styles; and here we have no way forward other than the inspection of potential examples in detail.

3. What should those who are worried do? Though this book offers little specific advice, here, for what it is worth, is a thought: treat our exemplars as
cautionary tales; keep reminding ourselves that we are all moral equals; and
cultivate a healthy sense of gratitude and responsibility to others. See also
"Letter to an Asshole."
4. The complex criteria for narcissistic personality disorder in the *Diagnostic
and Statistical Manual of Mental Disorders* are pretty good, if not quite definitive of the asshole. They include narcissists who aren't necessarily assholes,
such as what some call (in terms not found in the *DSM*) "piece of shit" narcissists, who suffer from a firm sense of inferiority. The asshole concept does
include what some call the "piece of gold" narcissist, who affirms his superiority over others, although that category might apply in other cases as well.

Our theory requires that the asshole be mistakenly entrenched in entitlement, but it is otherwise neutral about what sort of error he is making; he can be wrong about what he is entitled to in any number of ways for any number of reasons. It is thus an open question what the different styles of assholes are. This allows us to respect Aristotle's wise maxim that we should not expect precision from a theory beyond what its subject matter will bear. If poetry is not math, neither is virtue and vice. Still less so is the fluid variety of asshole vices. We thus proceed inductively, as Aristotle might. We examine an array of exemplars in hope that different asshole kinds will emerge.

BOORISH ASSHOLE

To begin, consider the asshole boor. A person can be boorish, insensitive, or rude without being an asshole; he might have good intentions and no sense of entitlement and yet be unable to read social cues. A boorish asshole, by contrast, is willfully insensitive to normal boundaries of courtesy or respect. He is usually out in the open about this, and even proud of that fact.

So, for example, Noel Gallagher of Oasis, in my view arguably the most self-consciously asshole rock band in history, trashes other artists seemingly just for the pleasure of mouthing off.[5] Radio host Rush Limbaugh is also conspicuously rude,

---

5. One blogger, who puts Noel Gallagher in his top four assholes in rock, cites his comments about members of rival band Blur (who should "catch AIDS and die"), Phil Collins ("the Antichrist"), Green Day (for plagiarizing "Wonderwall" in much the way Oasis plagiarizes other artists), and Radiohead ("at the end of the day people will always want to hear you play 'Creep.' Get over it. I never went to fucking university. I don't know what a paintbrush is; I never went to art school"). See http://brettwatts.blogspot.com/2008/05/top-4-assholes-in-rock_19.html.

but to enormous personal profit in money and political influence. Filmmaker Michael Moore is slightly more coy, dressing up sloppy treatment of his subjects in a cloak of social morality. In each of these cases, rudeness appears to be born not of mere insensitivity but of a sense of entitlement to set courtesy and respect aside. Gallagher seems to presume that pop success itself gives him license to do and say whatever he wants.[6] Both Limbaugh and Moore would presumably cite their greater causes, whether it is stopping the liberal menace (Limbaugh) or standing up for the workingman against corporate fat cats (Moore).[7]

A more subtle case is the influential early-twentieth-century American journalist, essayist, and critic H. L. Mencken. Here he is on presidents of the United States:

Woodrow Wilson: A "pedagogue gone mashugga."
Calvin Coolidge: The "intelligence of a lawn
    dog," his career "as appalling and as fas-
    cinating as a two-headed boy."
Herbert Hoover: "The perfect self-seeker. . . . His
    principles are so vague that even his intimates
    seem unable to put them into words, . . . He knows
    who his masters are, and he will serve them."

6. As Gallagher himself emphasizes in this interview at www.youtube.com/watch?v=YNe4qkfkLws. He claims he is not an asshole, even as he makes what could be seen as numerous asshole remarks.
7. To compare other boorish assholes, Ari Gold, from the television show *Entourage,* is gratuitously aggressive, much as Gallagher is. Gregory House, from the television show *House,* is aggressively rude but justifies this in the name of his manifest talent as a doctor in saving lives. His argument from moral cause seems more plausible than either Limbaugh's or Moore's, though he is still plainly an asshole.

> Warren G. Harding: "The master of a language in
> which the relations between word and mean-
> ing have long since escaped him. . . . [Harding's
> style] reminds me of a string of wet sponges; it
> reminds me of tattered washing on the wall . . .
> of stale bean soup, of college yells, of dogs bark-
> ing idiotically through endless nights. It is so
> bad that a sort of grandeur creeps into it."[8]

It is perhaps not a coincidence that Mencken celebrated
the philosopher Friedrich Nietzsche with the following praise:
"No epithet was too outrageous, no charge was too far-fetched,
no manipulation or interpretation of evidence was too daring, to
enter into his ferocious indictment."[9] Mencken would know; he
nicely described himself.

SMUG ASSHOLE

While a boorish asshole feels right in setting courtesy or respect
aside, he won't necessarily be smug about it. Indeed, he may
have nagging fears about his inadequacy and choose offense as
the best defense. The smug asshole, by contrast, is comfortable
in his sense that others are inferior, and indeed presumes that
others should well expect him to behave as their better.

Mencken's boorishness, for example, seems to reveal a settled confidence in his manifest intellectual superiority. Oxford

8. Collected by Robert Edwards at www.findagrave.com/cgi-bin/fg.cgi?page
=gr&GRid=706.
9. H. L. Mencken, "The Mailed Fist and Its Prophet," *The Atlantic,* November
1914, www.theatlantic.com/magazine/archive/1914/11/the-mailed-fist-and-its
-prophet/6393/.

biologist Richard Dawkins is similarly self-assured in his broad-side against theism and religious belief, *The God Delusion*.[10] He writes that the views of millions of reasonable and intelligent people (even if ultimately mistaken) have no merit whatsoever and appears to feel entitled to give sloppy treatment to arguments for the existence of God that have seriously engaged philosophers for thousands of years.[11] Larry Summers, who served in both the Clinton and Obama administrations and as president of Harvard University, betrays supreme self-confidence, even among his Harvard colleagues[12] and especially in policy disputes. Economist Andrew Metrick recalls a telling conversation with Summers:

> Larry was complaining about the position Treasury was taking on some issue, and how he couldn't dislodge them from their position, that they just wouldn't budge. I said, "Well, Larry, maybe, they're right." He just looked at me and said, "That's not an issue. I can win any argument. I can win arguing either side. But then I sit back and think, 'Which side did I win more soundly and fairly?' That's usually the right answer."[13]

10. Richard Dawkins, *The God Delusion* (London: Black Swan, 2007).

11. The book title is in my view arguably an asshole title—since it lacks a serious philosophical refutation of the existence of God of the sort that Dawkins is not, as a biologist, professionally qualified to provide.

12. One friend explains Summers's related view of salaries this way: "Larry felt that it didn't make sense that while he was being paid well by Harvard, some other professors were being paid in his ballpark. After all, he was Larry Summers, and who the hell were the rest of them?" See Ron Suskind, *Confidence Men: Wall Street, Washington, and the Education of a President* (New York: HarperCollins, 2011), 199.

13. Suskind, *Confidence Men*, 348–49.

For smugness, however, there is of course no place like France. It has graced us with the great asshole novelist Gustave Flaubert. (With carefully crafted pretentiousness, Flaubert writes: "Woman is a vulgar animal from whom man has created an excessively beautiful ideal"; "Read much, but not many books"; "Exuberance is better than taste"; "There is no truth. There is only perception.")[14] The tradition of *le smug asshole* has been vigilantly preserved up to our day. Arrogant, contemptuous of lesser races, humorless, completely unwilling to admit a mistake. *Et voilà!*, Bernard-Henri Lévy (or "BHL").

He is the modern-day, self-appointed Tocqueville, a "God is dead but my hair is perfect"[15] celebrity philosopher, who has recently written passionately in condemnation of the humiliating killing of Muammar Gaddafi:

> You can say that the man was a monster. You can replay again and again the scenes that for eight months have haunted the friends of free Libya—the images of mass executions, torture, the hangings of April 7, the prisoners who were sort of buried alive until released from their prisons by the revolution—these and so many other victims of the dictatorship. You can point out that Gaddafi had a hundred chances to negotiate, to stop it all, to save himself, and that, if he elected not to do so, if he preferred to bleed his people to the very end, he chose his fate knowingly. . . .

14. www.famousquotescollection.com/author/Gustave-Flaubert.
15. The phrase is due to Michael O'Donnell's "Another Frenchman Assesses Our Democracy," a review of Lévy's *American Vertigo: Traveling America in the Footsteps of Tocqueville, San Francisco Chronicle*, January 29, 2006, www .sfgate.com/cgi-bin/article.cgi?f=/c/a/2006/01/29/RVGHUGQ7341.DTL.

I don't buy it. I may be an incurable romantic, or what amounts to the same thing, an unreconstructed opponent of the absolute evil that I believe the death penalty to be. There is, in the spectacle of Gaddafi's lynching, something revolting.[16]

Except of course that BHL had only months before called unequivocally for the West to militarily overthrow Gaddafi and then crowed publicly that he had had a hand in making that happen. (He was the dapper diplomat in a top secret mission that involved commandeering a vegetable truck across the Libyan border for a clandestine rendezvous with Libyan rebel forces. A subsequent late-night satellite phone call to President Sarkozy spurred France into action).[17] While BHL had called for military action in previous conflicts, this one seems to have turned out unfortunately: How could he have expected that the guy would, you know, get killed? While he is clearly not so self-satisfied as to refuse to change his mind, he still seems quite satisfied with his dynamic, critical, metacritical, dialogical, persistent, relentless, self-proclamedly courageous posture of moral dissatisfaction. One can certainly appreciate his expressed humanitarian sentiment. One might even admire his voicing of moral outrage when no one else would, if he had forthrightly acknowledged a possible shift in his stance. Without that, we

16. Bernard-Henri Lévy, "A Moral Tipping Point: Bernard-Henri Lévy on the Unsettling Implications of Gaddafi's Gory End," *The Daily Beast,* October 23, 2011, www.thedailybeast.com/newsweek/2011/10/23/a-moral-tipping-point-on -gaddafi-s-gory-end.html.

17. James Crabtree, "Philosophes sans frontières as Plato Battles Nato," London *Financial Times,* April 1, 2011, www.ft.com/intl/cms/s/0/986a997e-5c8d -11e0-ab7c-00144feab49a.html#axzz1nXUYMxy1?

are left with moralistic smugness: a suggestion that the rest of us have been less than circumspect and now—unlike him—find ourselves complicit in an "absolute evil."

THE ASSHOLE BOSS

We have so far examined people who seem to act from a deep feature of their personalities, quite aside from their particular social station or role. Perhaps more common, however, are cases in which assholery is socially induced, or at least exposed, because the person is placed in a position of power.

The statement "My boss is *such* an asshole" has become something of a cliché. All too often it has an element of truth. For many people, a position of power becomes a standing license for privileges that do not necessarily come with the job—things such as barking orders when a polite request will do, routinely being late for staff meetings because of supposedly more pressing business, knowing that being the boss means never having to say "I'm sorry," regularly reminding all who is in power, and so on. When questions arise, the asshole boss has a ready answer, his all-purpose entitlement afforded by his instituted role: "Tough. I am the boss." But the asshole boss needn't be boorish or overtly abusive. There are of course famous examples of bosses who are, such as supermodel Naomi Campbell, who assaulted her housekeeper with a cell phone, or General George Patton, who slapped a wounded soldier while touring a war hospital (apparently to get him to shape up). More familiar nowadays, from film and TV, is the boss whose misguided sense of superiority taints routine dealings in the workplace, as with the condescension of Bill Lumbergh in the comedy *Office Space,* or with David Brent's excruciating insensitivity to his employees' feelings in the

British TV comedy *The Office,* or with the obnoxiousness and gross self-absorption of Michael Scott in the American version.

THE ROYAL ROYAL ASSHOLE

If roles can induce bad behavior, it makes sense that the minor tyrants of the workplace pale by comparison to the tyrant kings of old. Yet a true tyrant is immeasurably worse than an asshole, and in many cases the concept of an asshole will not apply. A king, after all, *has* a standing institutional entitlement to do as he pleases: he's the king. The grotesque manipulative villainy of, say, Shakespeare's Richard III is closer to what we now call a psychopath than to the proper asshole.

Henry VIII, king of England, does, however, seem to qualify. He broke from the pope in Rome and appointed himself head of the English Church for the worthy cause of divorcing his wife, Catherine (or, as British nationalists now put it, for "putting England first"). Despite strict conventional limits on divorce and remarriage, he managed to marry six women, divorcing two and putting two to death (with his third wife dying in childbirth). Henry was not, however, a pure tyrant; he always avoided summary-style edicts and at least gave executions a pretext of legality. He was genuinely concerned for procedure, which is precisely why he doggedly sought to have his divorce from Catherine publicly endorsed by his loyal chancellor, Sir Thomas More. More, an honest and devout Catholic, famously would not play ball. And although Henry would eventually arrange More's execution on perjured charges of high treason, this was a last-ditch measure taken only after he persistently tried to bring More around. As Robert Bolt's *A Man for All Seasons* portrays Henry's plea to More, Henry the king is reduced to a mad asshole, abruptly alternating between respectful appeals to friendship and towering rage. In one moment he thunders at the top of his lungs, "They that say she is my wife are not only liars, but traitors! Yes, traitors! That I will not brook. Treachery! It maddens me! It is a deadly canker in the body politic, and I will have it out!" A moment later he gently comments, "See? You see how you've maddened me. I hardly know myself." Henry senses the sovereignty of another man's conscience and mind and so to some extent appreciates the boundaries of respectful entreaty. He then flies through those boundaries—only to again feel their force as something beyond his powers. Henry was accustomed to getting what he wanted and felt he had every right to bully More into changing his mind. But he also respected More and wanted an honest change of mind, something even a king cannot summon by his mere command. Henry seems less like a pure tyrant and more like an asshole to the extent he at once transgresses and pays respects to a higher moral law.[18]

THE PRESIDENTIAL ASSHOLE

If the asshole king is something of a limiting case, the asshole boss of the workplace stands at the other end of a spectrum: his role is often fairly well defined. Between these poles stand most heads of state. We do not any longer accord unchecked power to our leaders. Yet there remains considerable latitude for inter-

---

18. Here we might compare Edward VIII, who abdicated the throne within a year to marry an American divorcée. Although he was spoiled and self-indulgent, and lacked any sense of duty to his country, he does not qualify as an asshole in our sense, since he did not seem to act from entitlement, not even the royal institutional entitlements at his disposal.

pretation of what high office puts within one's rightful power. The presidential asshole goes beyond what is, morally speaking, within his rights.

A glaring example is the outrageous speechifying regularly delivered before the United Nations by presidents Hugo Chavez of Venezuela and Mahmoud Ahmadinejad of Iran. To the chagrin of the diplomats who regularly leave the General Assembly meeting room in protest, as well as many of the citizens whom Chavez or Ahmadinejad speaks in the name of, this is strictly consistent with General Assembly rules that allocate speaking time; they do, alas, have the right to speak. But rights can be held and exercised in different ways, and the right to speak does not entitle one to flagrantly violate diplomatic protocol and norms of courtesy. Chavez and Ahmadinejad are presidential assholes because they manufacture bad reasons (e.g., their oppression by Western powers) as to why they are entitled to set those obligations aside.

Which is not to say true leadership won't sometimes require pushing conventional boundaries. Winston Churchill had the huge ego of a man who does large things, as, for example, when he led England into a disastrous battle at Gallipoli with defiant incompetence. He later successfully rallied Britain in a brave and risky stand against the Third Reich, and not by being a gentle man. He is known for his rude quips (for instance: Bessie Braddock: "Sir, you are drunk." Churchill: "Madam, you are ugly. In the morning, I shall be sober"). He was sometimes unprincipled (he changed parties for opportunistic reasons). And he was exceedingly demanding with his staff, always putting his own needs first. Yet he also had a tremendous sense of humor and a soft side. He wept publicly when he toured the cities bombed during the war. And he inspired loyalty and affection in almost everyone who worked for him. Churchill was boorish, but he was not quite an asshole.

American president George W. Bush was also bold, and even bolder in breaking established rules. He arguably rejected international law in the matter of prisoners of war, and he dramatically shifted the delicate balance of governmental powers toward the executive branch. Is Bush akin to Churchill? History, so far, has not been so kind. Yet Bush, the man himself, probably is not an asshole.[19] There is an element of truth in the cliché that he's a regular guy, the kind of guy you'd like to have a beer with. While he is perhaps insensitive, and some would say dull (mistakenly, I would say), he is not immunized against the complaints of others; he'd hear them out over that beer. Insofar as the charge of assholism applies to the Bush administration, it is because of serious assholes such as his vice president, Dick Cheney, who often ignored Bush and simply did as he pleased. (We will return to Cheney momentarily.)

If Bush was willing to take huge risks and boldly cross bright lines, the unavoidable contrast is President Barack Obama, who has been cautious by comparison, even tame. The man is not an asshole, and indeed something of an antiasshole. For many progressives, this is a problem, as we can see from their objections: he pulls back in using the powers he clearly has;

19. Hugo Chavez called Bush an asshole on the implausible grounds that he heeded advice from "imperialist" aides to support a 2002 coup against him. "He was an asshole to believe them," Chavez said at a rally in Caracas. See Patrick Markey, "Chavez Calls Bush 'Asshole' as Foes Fight Troops," February 29, 2004, www.washingtonpost.com/wp-dyn/articles/A17578-2004Feb29 .html. Merely believing someone or heeding their advice—whether good or bad—is hardly sufficient to make someone into an asshole. Perhaps presidential responsibilities in an important decision require not believing too readily. But believing, per se, would not suffice.

he fails to respond to the opposition, allowing it to define the debate; he is too eager to listen, to understand, so as not to offend, to the point of being dragged away from his convictions by people stubborn in theirs; he makes preemptive concessions in approaching the bargaining table and then further concessions down the line; he favors compromised policies that absorb everyone's concerns and do much less good than they could. In short, progressives wish Obama could behave a lot more like an asshole.[20] Yet it is not clear—at least not as yet (campaign season aside)—that Obama is willing, or even able, to do that. He just may not be that kind of guy.[21]

We might say, in short, that progressives wish Obama would be more like presidential candidate Newt Gingrich. As much as or more than anyone, Gingrich created the United States' polarized political climate. As Speaker of the House, he ordered Republican lawmakers to stay home much of the week in order to avoid forming bipartisan relationships and a sense of common cause with Democrats, and he championed the strategy of seeking to dominate Democrats even at the expense of things both parties agree about. These are asshole moves—things an asshole would do—to the extent we think legislators are obligated to address common problems, especially where they can

---

20. Beltway insiders apparently distinguish between aggressive campaigning, aimed at scoring points against the opponent, and a "dick move," which crosses some fine line. Such moves put one a step in the direction of being an asshole while stopping short. To pull dick moves systematically would move one into asshole territory, as in "What a dick, what an asshole!"

21. However, no one has ever accused Obama's former chief of staff, Rahm Emanuel, of being an antiasshole. For discussion, see Matt Taibbi, "Supreme Court of Assholedom: Rahm Emanuel et al.," March 4, 2011, www.rollingstone .com/politics/blogs/taibblog/supreme-court-rulings-daniel-snyder-rahm -emanuel-elton-john-et-al-20110304.

agree, in which case they are not entitled to put politics first and last. Many will disagree with that moral assessment and so take a more favorable view of Gingrich's political tactics, and indeed the use of certain tactics alone would not make Gingrich, the man, an asshole per se. Even his having an affair while his wife was in the hospital with cancer (or any of his several other affairs, in other marriages) wouldn't *necessarily* put him in the asshole camp; he could just lack self-control. Likewise with his rude comment, about that same wife, that "she isn't young enough or pretty enough to be the president's wife. And besides, she has cancer"; he may simply be petty, tactless, and rude. He is an asshole, however, if he does such things out of a misguided sense that he has encompassing rights to them. Or as he puts it, in his own words: "I think you can write a psychological profile of me that says I found a way to immerse my insecurities in a cause large enough to justify whatever I wanted it to."[22]

Still, in general, what we ultimately make of a head of state has less to do with his or her personal dispositions than with the justifiability of what he or she is trying to do. We do in fact give leaders wide latitude when, but only when, we feel clearly they are acting from a credible vision of the greater good. Where we differ over whether the vision is credible or good and how far one should go in its name, we naturally differ over who is and who is not an asshole.

22. Gail Sheehy, "The Inner Quest of Newt Gingrich," *Vanity Fair,* September 1995, www.pbs.org/wgbh/pages/frontline/newt/vanityfair1.html. Not that he seems terribly insecure when he explains, "I think grandiose thoughts," comparing himself favorably to great American leaders such as Abraham Lincoln and Henry Clay. See Alana Goodman, "Gingrich's 'Grandiose Thoughts,'" *Commentary,* January 20, 2012, www.commentarymagazine.com/2012/01/20/gingrich-grandiose-thoughts/.

Except, of course, when it is abundantly clear that there is no such sense of greater cause. Former Italian prime minister Silvio Berlusconi is therefore our paradigmatic asshole of public life, and for good reason: the Italian public good was never at the top of his concerns. Showing that it is not at the top of his concerns is one of his top concerns (he called himself a "part-time prime minister"). We for years heard lurid tales of parties and underage prostitutes; of embezzlement, fraud, and judges bribed; of laws passed to protect him from prosecution and promote his business ventures, usually followed by a Berlusconi charm offensive. Berlusconi was not ashamed and clearly felt entitled to all of this, despite the fact that many Italians reviled him and felt deeply ashamed of the spectacle. It is not that rationalizations are offered but they are flimsy ones; no attempt at rationalization is even made. That seems to be Berlusconi's point: he pillages Italian public life for private gain, out in the open, not because it is right but because he can.

Berlusconi's best line of defense is to spread blame. How did he survive for so long? Aside from having loyal deputies, the answer, it seems, is that enough of the Italian public supported him, let him get away with it, and even encouraged him to go on. All he did, one might add, is to masterfully follow a long tradition of rule Italian style, as received from Mussolini's bombastic fascism; from the Machiavellian, Mafia-connected machinations of seven-time prime minister Giulio Andreotti (also known as "Beelzebub"); and from Massimiliano Cencelli's carefully crafted "manual" for dividing up political spoils. Berlusconi might thus lay solemn claim to have inherited rightful fascist dictatorial powers and then ask, with a flashing smile: Is it not good to be the king? The trouble with this argument is that Italy is now a democracy, which itself makes Berlusconi not royalty but corrupt.[23] His royalty is at most the royalty enjoyed by assholes of a special royal kind.[24]

THE CORPORATE ASSHOLE

Although the argument from culture won't help Berlusconi, it nevertheless does contain a general insight: the asshole in power is *shaped* by his position and its culture as much as he shapes it. Much as with our ordinary asshole boss, assholes may wind up in power, not simply because assholes are especially prone to seek it out but because the position induces a creeping sense of entitlement in those who come to occupy the role. It is said that power corrupts. We may add that it brings out the inner asshole, by deadening one's capacities of empathy and understanding, telling one there is no need to listen, and beckoning one into egocentricism and easy rationalization of ever-widening privileges. The asshole boss simply settles into a firm sense that "I'm the boss," which gradually becomes a firm sense that "I'm the man" in traffic, at the post office, and at his child's soccer game.[25]

23. But was Berlusconi in sufficient control of the media such that the public discourse needed for a functioning democracy just wasn't there? Might this mean that he was not corrupting a democracy but rather preserving the fascist order of old (much as Mussolini did by manipulating the public through mass communication)? I doubt it, but there is perhaps an argument to have here.
24. Not to mention that Italy has its share of distinguished political thinkers and leaders. Along with the corrupt figures mentioned in the text, Tony Barber, in his incisive "Why Italy Is Short of Statesmen but Long on Scoundrels," notes upstanding figures such as Antonio Gramsci, Benedetto Croce, Piero Gobetti, Alcide De Gasperi, Carlo Azeglio Ciampi, and Giorgio Napolitano. See London *Financial Times*, September 23, 2011, www.ft.com/intl/cms/s/0/1ecf9cfa-e481-11e0-92a3-00144feabdc0.html#axzz1oAZQSAus?
25. See also "Asshole Even Shoots Pool Like an Asshole," *The Onion*, January 15,

We should therefore be skeptical of journalist Jon Ronson's striking claim that psychopaths are rare in society but relatively common in the corporate boardroom.[26] More likely, the board-room is flush with assholes. Corporate culture spawns them.

A boardroom asshole is not to be confused with the quite welcome "shit" or SOB ("shits on boards"), who goes for the decisive objection, who can't hide a strong opinion, and who might have just hurt someone's feelings but, all told, helps the group meet its goals.[27] And we should admit that there probably are a few corporate psychopaths, such as "Chainsaw Al" Dunlap, who relished mass layoffs and the rewards heaped upon him by investors, seemingly with no concern for the resulting human toll and perhaps with delight in the exercise of power. The mark of the psychopath, as we will understand him, is to have for-sworn, or perhaps never fully acquired, the use of moral concepts (perhaps because of childhood abuse).[28] The psychopath merely *feigns* moral action, usually to create the trust needed to effectively manipulate others. The asshole, by contrast, traf-

2003, www.onionsportsnetwork.com/articles/asshole-even-shoots-pool-like-an -asshole,2938/.

26. Jon Ronson, *The Psychopath Test: A Journey Through the Madness Industry* (New York: Riverhead, 2011).

27. Lucy Kellaway, "Everyone Benefits from a Beast in the Boardroom," Lon-don *Financial Times,* October 9, 2011, www.ft.com/intl/cms/s/0/3bdb9b68 -f0cb-11e0-aec8-00144feab49a.html#axzz1oAZQSAus?.

28. Here we follow moral philosopher Gary Watson's reading of the psycho-logical evidence, "The Trouble with Psychopaths," in *Reasons and Recognition: Essays on the Philosophy of T. M. Scanlon,* eds. R. Jay Wallace, Rahul Kumar, and Samuel Freeman (New York: Oxford University Press, 2011). Psychopathy is thus not mere "empathy erosion," as according to Cambridge psychologist Simon Baron-Cohen in *The Science of Evil: On Empathy and the Origins of Cruelty* (New York: Basic Books, 2011). It is a specific way empathy might be eroded.

fics in and is moved by moral justification—except that moral justification, for him, leads to an entrenched sense of special entitlement. He gets upset precisely because he feels entitled to special advantage, especially, he'll say, in light of the good he does. Thus Steve Jobs's knowledge of how much people love his gadgets could potentially explain why he felt entitled to park in handicapped spaces, skimp on philanthropic giving,[29] and intentionally hurt his associates. As Jobs's best friend, Jony Ive, explains, "when he's very frustrated . . . his way to achieve catharsis is to hurt somebody. And I think he feels he has a liberty and license to do that. The normal rules of social engagement, he feels, don't apply to him."[30]

This moral sensibility makes all the difference for how assholes could emerge in boardrooms and grow in numbers over time. Psychopaths are not typically guided by social expectations. They see expectations not as potential moral commands but as mere regular patterns of behavior, as among so many billiard balls shifting around, that provide obstacles or opportunities for self-interested action. People are, in effect, regarded as mere things. Because psychopaths are unresponsive to expectations,

29. Even after a prematurely published obituary commented that he was miserly as regards charity, Jobs, having resumed control of Apple, ended the firm's philanthropic ventures. The thought was apparently that the firm could make great products and therefore have no further obligations to society. Yet it does not seem that providing gadget orgasms and access to computers for any number of people justifies not supporting worthy causes, at a small relative cost, that might benefit large numbers of people who are vastly worse off (causes such as malaria eradication, diabetes treatment, water tank construction, and so on).

30. Dylan Love, "16 Examples of Steve Jobs Being a Huge Jerk," *Business Insider,* October 25, 2011, www.businessinsider.com/steve-jobs-jerk-2011 -10#why-was-jobs-such-a-rude-person-16.

a culture of expectations, as it evolves over time, will probably fail to affect the overall population of psychopaths. As we will see further in chapter 6, however, the asshole's reasoning is shaped by the moral justifications his surrounding culture makes available to him. And so corporate culture can influence both net asshole production and the quality of whatever assholes get made.

Depending on the culture, then, an asshole can be better behaved or worse behaved than a psychopath. A healthy culture of corporate responsibility—to employee, consumer, and investor alike—can significantly limit how far an asshole will go in, say, firing workers to maximize both quarterly returns for investors and his personal compensation. In such a culture, even a proper asshole might not ruthlessly institute mass layoffs, let alone take pleasure in the exercise of power. At the same time, a different, perhaps ultracompetitive culture might unleash the asshole within. That would, for example, explain a recent study at the Swiss University of St. Gallen that tested egotism and the readiness to cooperate of stock traders as compared to psychopaths. In computer simulations and intelligence tests, the share traders behaved more recklessly and were more manipulative than the psychopaths. They showed a special concern for competitive dominance. As study coauthor Thomas Noll explained, "It was most important to the traders to get more than their opponents. . . . They spent a lot of energy trying to damage their opponents." As Noll elaborates, it was as though their neighbor had the same car, and "they took after it with a baseball bat so they could look better themselves."[31] The ultracompetitive

---

31. Spiegel Online, "Going Rogue: Share Traders More Reckless Than Psychopaths, Study Shows," *Der Spiegel*, September 26, 2011, www.spiegel.de/international/zeitgeist/0,1518,788462,00.html.

stock trading ethos, it seems, was carried over into how the traders played laboratory games. And would anyone be surprised to see it crop up elsewhere?

Accordingly, once the right (or the wrong) culture settles in, the asshole population can expand. Consider, for instance, the expectation that corporations are required to maximize shareholder value, because they have a "fiduciary duty to investors." If this is really a *duty* only to *investors*, it follows that there is a duty to *minimize* benefits, overall, to consumers and workers—that is to say, a *duty* to offer the bare minimum incentive required to get them to buy a product or show up to work. Many corporate heads will pull back from this, sensing that something is amiss. (Perhaps they ask: Isn't the rising tide of capitalism supposed to lift all boats and not just investor yachts?) The asshole CEO will embrace his duty with moral gusto, sensing an otherwise forbidden rush of power and profits lying ahead. (Thus even Chainsaw Al might not be a psychopath but simply a raging asshole.) Others who are not already assholes will nevertheless get comfortable with this behavior, trying to keep up with or beat the pack. As this is repeated across thousands of boardrooms and CEO offices, being steadily reinforced with oft-repeated suggestions of how all this works to the "greater good," assholes grow and flower. The way of the asshole can thus become the normal way.

But might this mean that, eventually, the asshole concept does not apply? Once enough people are doing something, it becomes a form of cooperation with the established way of doing things, not a *breach* of cooperative expectations. Should we say, then, that bankers, for example, are not assholes but simply good businessmen? Not necessarily. We suggest why when we examine the delusional asshole in chapter 3.

THE RECKLESS ASSHOLE

While many assholes shaped by their enabling cultures will push their entitlements only so far, others go a long way in the direction of the psychopath in terms of their lack of concern for great injury to life and limb and yet without wholly abandoning moral concern. An asshole in power may be reckless in the face of obviously grave risks precisely because he finds easy comfort in a sense of entitlement afforded by his larger moral cause. He may be culpably overconfident in his judgment about when his cause is best served, and so not especially circumspect about risks being imposed upon others. The neoconservative warriors, such as Dick Cheney, Donald Rumsfeld, Paul Wolfowitz, and Richard Perle, arguably so qualify, for having undertaken the Iraq invasion in the name of spreading liberty throughout the world but without a lot of attention to how this was supposed to work and so without a plan for the reconstruction of Iraq.

Cheney, in particular, might be viewed in these terms from an older-style conservative's perspective. According to many conservatives, his policies were a frontal assault on institutions that embody the wisdom of the ages. His doctrine of unlimited presidential power threatened to destabilize the delicate balance among coequal branches of government, while the doctrine of preventive war and the suspension of due process upended standing international treaty and customary law. Even so, he felt entitled to set aside the wisdom of the ages without fear and trembling, without the humble knowledge, well taught by Edmund Burke, that sweeping policy change may easily have unintended consequences that make the cure worse than the disease—for instance, anarchy in the wake of a quick invasion in Iraq.[32]

We find a more specific example of reckless disregard in the summer of 2002, while President Bush was only considering the decision to go to war with Iraq. In a speech to the Veterans of Foreign Wars, Vice President Cheney made a strong case for war against Saddam Hussein, which allies of the United States took as a definitive indication that Bush had already decided to go to war without consulting them. This in effect undermined U.S. efforts to make a case for war at the U.N. a few months later; the United States naturally seemed to be just going through the motions. Perhaps most strikingly, Cheney gave the speech after circumventing the usual procedures for "clearing" a speech with the president, the CIA, and other parties within the government, so that all are comfortable with its content. Cheney clearly decided that he was exempt from basic institutional obligations, and with great consequence for his president, his country, and for the world.

THE SELF-AGGRANDIZING ASSHOLE

One could qualify as a reckless asshole simply for gross negligence. As this last example suggests, Dick Cheney is also

32. Although we focus on the way Cheney holds his political views, the hunting accident in which he shot his own friend at least suggests an affinity with his personal conduct. Further evidence of personal entitlement (though not of recklessness) is Cheney's explanation of why he avoided Vietnam: "I had other priorities in the '60s than military service." While wanting to avoid war is understandable, and the remark could have been self-mocking, it does suggest that he set himself apart. What draftee didn't have other priorities? See www .slate.com/articles/news_and_politics/chatterbox/2004/03/elizabeth_cheney _deferment_baby.html.

self-aggrandizing, in the sense that he acted to enhance his own power, even to the point of usurping Bush's office. The self-aggrandizing asshole invokes moral cause, but his cause is ultimately, on balance, himself.

In Cheney's defense, we can at least say that he is a long-serving public official, who can offer a raft of sincere moral arguments for his policy views. Those are arguments we can seriously engage, quite aside from Cheney's political tactics. The wild-eyed arguments of Chavez and Ahmadinejad are harder to take seriously and difficult to even grasp. This makes them self-aggrandizing assholes of a purer style. Yet there is a general similarity (even if we finally judge such cases quite differently). Chavez and Ahmadinejad presumably do have some intelligible grievances, even if they are inconclusive in the final analysis (after all, the major powers hardly have a spotless history in Latin American and Middle Eastern relations). In general, then, self-aggrandizing assholes seem to come in a broad spectrum of pure and less pure styles, depending on how motives of enhancing their own power mix with other moral concerns.

Perhaps an especially pure case is Huey Long, the early 1930s' Louisiana governor and U.S. senator. Though he shared President Franklin Delano Roosevelt's progressive outlook, albeit from Roosevelt's left, Roosevelt regarded him as one of the two most dangerous men in America (the other being Douglas MacArthur) for his corrupt and demagogic politics.[33] Long claimed to be moved by moral concern, as when he condemned the inequalities of his day ("Not a single thin dime of concentrated, bloated, pompous wealth, massed in the hands of a few people, has been raked down to relieve the masses"),[34] and indeed he criticized the U.S. political system in terms that resonate today ("They've got a set of Republican waiters on one side and set of Democratic waiters on the other side, but no matter which set of waiters brings you the dish, the legislative grub is all prepared in the same Wall Street kitchen").[35] As for political tactics, however, Long felt entitled to take any means, without being especially concerned about whether they really were necessary for his ends, or whether they were appropriate in a democracy. As he put it, "I'd rather violate every one of the damn conventions and see my bills passed, than sit back in my office, all nice and proper, and watch 'em die."[36] "I used to try to get things done by saying 'please.' . . . Now . . . I dynamite 'em out of my path."[37] When he was accused of demagoguery, he in effect ignored the moral issue of *how* power is exercised in a democratic society with this convenient definition: "I would describe a demagogue as a politician who don't keep his promises."[38] In effect, Long justified his political machine by defining corruption out of existence.

On the left in our own day, a less extreme example of moralized self-aggrandizing might be U.S. presidential candidate Ralph Nader, whose spoiler role helped to usher in what other progressives regard as the disastrous years of George W. Bush. Or one might think of former U.S. senator John Edwards, who

34. T. Harry Williams, *Huey Long* (New York: Alfred A. Knopf, 1969), 708.
35. Williams, *Huey Long,* 589.
36. Williams, *Huey Long,* 298.
37. Michael E. Parrish, *Anxious Decades: America in Prosperity and Depression, 1920–1941* (New York: Norton, 1994), 164.
38. Richard D. White, Jr., *Kingfish: The Reign of Huey P. Long* (New York: Random House, 2006), 248.

seemed to feel that his purported concern for American poverty itself justified his presidential run. Did it somehow make up for his secret unfaithfulness to his cancer-afflicted wife and the risk that a successful bid would eventually be undermined when news of the secret affair surfaced, at a huge loss to the political left? Or was he mainly concerned to augment his own power? The answer seems at best unclear. Similarly, WikiLeaks founder Julian Assange invokes high principles of transparency in letting the public know what governments are up to. But the unprincipled and reckless way he exposes diplomatic confidences suggests that he is equally if not mainly concerned with being in a position to do a lot of damage. If he does have moral motives, his smug sense of being above accountability tips the scales of self-aggrandizement the other way.

Still more complicated are British imperialists such as Cecil Rhodes, Lord Kitchener, and General Gordon of Khartoum. They operated within a political culture that supplied ready moral justifications for promoting Britain's power around the world. Even John Stuart Mill, one of the great progressives of the era, infamously approved of the colonial subjugation of "barbarians."[39] Only after being properly civilized, presumably in good English style, could they become fit for self-rule. Mill genuinely believed this was for the barbarians' own good (and he was not an asshole). But a culture in which paternalistic colonialism was widely accepted of course made it easy for others to seize the opportunities for power from less pure motives.

Cecil Rhodes is a notorious exemplar. Even in his own day, Rhodes was apparently "revered by his intimates, who regarded him as a towering colossus," but also "reviled by those who saw

---

39. John Stuart Mill, *On Liberty*, 2nd ed. (London: J. W. Parker and Son, 1859), 23.

him as an unprincipled and unscrupulous adventurer."[40] He was ruthless, corrupt, and immensely greedy in opening up diamond mines in South Africa, acting from a sense of both impunity and imperial license. Rhodes also had a tremendous sense of mission. He dreamed of a railroad spanning Africa from Cape Town to Cairo and ultimately hoped the Anglo-Saxon race would dominate the whole earth, with rebellious America eventually returning to the empire (and with America's best and brightest coming on Rhodes Scholarships to England in the meanwhile).

This turned out to be somewhat overly optimistic. Entitlement born of cosmic grandiosity caught on well in America. Oil baron John D. Rockefeller was apparently enriched not because Wild West American capitalism gave him free rein but because, as he put it without apology, "God gave me my money."[41] An earlier generation was similarly moved by the asshole doctrine of Manifest Destiny, through the westward expansion and beyond, to sweep aside native peoples in their path. Although America was a late comer in the global competition for subjugation rights over foreign peoples, it did have a crack at Cuba, Puerto Rico, and the Philippines in 1898. Though the stakes were relatively small, Albert J. Beveridge, in a campaign for the Indiana Senate, saw in the United States "a greater England with a nobler destiny." In particular, the United States was, he said:

> a mighty people that He has planted on this soil; a people sprung from the most masterful blood of history; a people perpetually revitalized by the virile, man-producing

40. "Cecil Rhodes," in *The Oxford Dictionary of National Biography* (Oxford: Oxford University Press, 2004).
41. www.bartleby.com/73/1207.html.

working-folk of all the earth; a people imperial by virtue
of their power, by right of their institutions, by authority of
their Heaven-directed purposes—the propagandists and
not the misers of liberty.[42]

Beveridge of course then naturally pressed the question:
"Shall the American people continue their march toward the
commercial supremacy of the world?" To answer "no," he went
on to explain, would make one "an infidel to American power
and practical sense." It would be to withhold the gift of our talents from the world, "to rot in our own selfishness." Nor would
there be a point in asking for consent from a people now incapable of self-government; we already know they would gladly
accept: "Would not the people of the Philippines prefer the just,
human, civilizing government of this Republic to the savage,
bloody rule of pillage and extortion from which we have rescued
them?" (meaning colonial rule by Spain).

Now, even the progressive Mill seriously advanced similar arguments from liberty, incapacity of self-governance, and
benevolent duty. As uncomfortable as they are for us to contem-
plate today, one can at least understand the logic behind Mill's
view. But Beveridge also trumpets Manifest Destiny, a doctrine
that is asshole in its purest form. That is, it is not just a mistaken
justification but mainly a way of refusing to engage the potential objections of others. Imagine, by way of illustration, how it
would play in an attempt by Beveridge to justify colonial subjec-
tion to a representative Filipino.

42. Albert Beveridge, "The March of the Flag," in *The Meaning of the Times*
(Indianapolis: Bobbs-Merrill Company, 1908; repr. 1968). The quotations in
the text below are also from this speech.

Filipino: It seems like you guys are trying to take
over. Might I ask why you think that is okay?

Beveridge: It is manifest that our destiny is to rule
over you.

Filipino: Really, that isn't quite manifest to us. Is
it that you are somehow *forced,* perhaps by
God, to come all this way to our shores?

Beveridge: No, we aren't forced; we are right,
right because we plainly *will* rule over you.

Filipino: Sorry, I'm not following. Isn't the question between us *why* you have a right to rule,
and, in particular, why this is *plainly* true?

Beveridge: It *is* plainly true. You just don't get it, do
you? I wouldn't expect understanding from a
savage.

In fact, the Filipinos did eventually make their preference
clear. Realizing that the United States was merely replacing
Spain as a new imperial power, they kept up the war for political independence. But this of course gave the colonialist little
pause; he had no interest in listening. As Kipling would explain,
Filipino resistance only strengthens the call of duty to "take up
the White Man's burden," to "Go bind your sons to exile / To
serve your captives' need / To wait in heavy harness / On flut-
tered folk and wild—Your new-caught, sullen peoples / Half
devil and half child."[43]

It is hard to say whether the American doctrines of Manifest Destiny and exceptionalism became thinner and thinner as

43. Rudyard Kipling, "The White Man's Burden," 1899.

rationalizations, over time, than the original British arguments for imperialism. The clear common element is reinforcement of a cosmic entitlement to do pretty objectionable things without a lot of circumspection—assholery and more on a world-historical scale.

[3] NEWER ASSHOLE STYLES

The assholes we have so far canvassed largely share a thick sense of moral entitlement. Just as hypocrisy is the homage that vice pays to virtue, Rhodes, Beveridge, and Rockefeller all felt a need to invoke entitlement on a cosmic scale, in effect sensing that something might be majorly amiss. In stark contrast with the grandiose reasoning of the era of colonialism, the asshole in more recent modern life often requires little or no pretext of larger cause for the special privileges he feels entitled to enjoy. He will usually have some sort of rationalization ready at hand—he is not the psychopath who rejects moral concepts altogether—but the rationalizations are becoming ever thinner, ever more difficult to identify. This newer, purer style of asshole often just presumes he should enjoy special privileges in social life as a matter of course and so requires little by way of reason for taking them as the opportunity arises.

The older style of asshole is comparatively easy to sort into types, according to their different thick entitlements. To the extent we can identify a definite moral outlook and confidently reject it as wrong, we can even take comfort in our sense of clarity about how the asshole goes awry. The newer style of asshole is more disquieting because he is harder to pin down. His thinned-out and shifting rationalizations won't necessarily settle into any particular sustained moral perspective that we can confidently identify and challenge as wrong. Instead, his sense of entitlement is mainly identifiable in functional terms, as the stable disposition to come up with some such rationalizations or other, as the situation requires. This chapter will nevertheless try to get a range of key examples under some kind of intellectual control. Because the newer breed of asshole is harder to pin down, we will pay even greater attention to the details of our exemplars, if only to illustrate that there is indeed a newer, thinner, and purer asshole style. (And, again, where you don't share my moral and political opinions, you might think of different examples of the same general type.)

SELF-AGGRANDIZING ASSHOLE
WITH THIN MORAL PRETEXT

Chapter 2 mentioned several examples of self-aggrandizement in the name of a larger moral cause. The newer style of self-aggrandizing asshole needs little or no such pretext. Jerry Falwell, for example, hardly missed an opportunity to seize the limelight with catchy comments about Jews (who "can make more money accidentally than you can on purpose"); Martin Luther King (of questionable sincerity given "left-wing associations"); Muslims ("Mohammed was a terrorist"); or homosexuals ("AIDS is not just God's punishment for homosexuals, it is God's punishment for the society that tolerates homosexuals"). All this was presumably supposed to have something to do with the humble name of Jesus of Nazareth, something that allowed Falwell, as a prominent evangelical Christian, to feel justified in saying things few thinking people would say. What that something was, or could have been, was never quite clear, and Falwell did not seem especially inclined to publicly explain how it comported with Christian charity, the love of truth, and the rejection of pride, if a potential conflict even occurred to him. What he mainly cared about, it seems, was being on the air.[1]

Donald Trump plainly likes being on the air. He is convincingly portrayed as an asshole in the documentary *Small Potatoes: Who Killed the USFL?* (answer: Trump, as one man's greed and ego brought down a whole sports league). Lately, however, Trump has become something closer to a media buffoon—except that he does not seem to be joking. Like Falwell, Trump believes there is something important in his appearing and reappearing in the news and on TV, without betraying any sense that a lot of us have a hard time seeing what that important something would be.[2]

In Trump's defense, it may be said that he is merely an "ass-clown"[3] or, still more charitably, an elder master of the attention-getting game now played daily by the Facebook youth. He may in that regard seem a role model, an accomplished media entrepreneur, and while this isn't quite a public service, it is at least the kind of thing modern society loves. In a culture of narcissism, you don't need any special reason to lay claim to the attention of others; you simply get attention

1. Falwell did eventually defend civil rights for gays (as an "American value," "not a liberal or conservative value"). Could this have reflected a change of heart? Many assholes do ease up as death approaches. We can hope so for Falwell, even if he never did publicly repent.

2. Some might consider Trump's getting President Obama to release the long form of his birth certificate a blow for justice, as Trump does. In that case, one could count this morally motivated act as an exception that proves the rule; Trump doesn't normally act from a sense of higher cause, even if he did in this one case.

3. Which appears to be some combination of being a "clown" and being an "ass," but perhaps without the entrenched sense of entitlement that we take as the mark of the asshole.

as you can, as anyone else of course would ("if you don't flaunt it, you don't got it," to reverse a familiar saying). On the other hand, if we find our current zeitgeist mistaken, on the grounds that laying claim to the attention of others *does* require good enough reasons—whether for the sake of modesty or just for the sake of not adding to the deafening contemporary media noise machine—then we can view narcissistic attention seeking as a way of acting like an asshole. Our narcissistic age thus might help explain why assholes seem to be everywhere of late.

THE CABLE NEWS ASSHOLE

With the invention of twenty-four-hour TV news cycles, the wonders of technological change have created assholes specifically designed for TV. The cable news asshole is self-aggrandizing but not purely so; there is a slight pretext of service there. While few of them nowadays would pretend to be engaged in distinguished public service in the fourth estate, many will say they are really pleased to be giving people what they want.

People apparently want to listen to blowhards. Thus Chris Matthews has a popular show on MSNBC. The faux blowhard Stephen Colbert on Comedy Central blows harder, except that Matthews is not staging a ruse. He traffics in attention-grabbing—every day is D-day intensity, even when he is saying little of consequence, as though little or no reason to claim our attention were required. Another left-leaning bloviator, Keith Olbermann, at least offers moral outrage as grounds for our concern, even as he is a worse asshole for feeling entitled to set aside any sense of measure in making outrageous, indulgent moral criticisms.[4]

---

4. Thus the element of truth in Ben Affleck's *SNL* spoof (see www.nbc.com/saturday-night-live/video/countdown-with-keith-olbermann/805561/). On a

When it comes to cable news assholes, however, we need not bother to attempt evenhandedness between left and right. The right-leaning version of being "fair and balanced"—that is, Fox News—is our gold standard. It pioneered the genre; it dominates in viewers, ratings, and profits; and it leads the way in innovation of the new asshole styles. We therefore pause to dwell on the case.

Neil Cavuto, a Fox News host, was actually called an asshole on the air. Here is an exchange from his show about fiscal stimulus and its relation to job creation with the mild-mannered AFL-CIO chief economist Ron Blackwell:

Ron Blackwell: Why don't you let me finish my thought?

Neil Cavuto: You never answer a basic question.

Blackwell: I'm answering you right now.

Cavuto: Why will spending work?

Blackwell: These programs created jobs but not net creation. We lost more jobs because of the recession than were created by these programs.

Neil Cavuto: Wait a minute, Ron. You're the chief economist there. Where did you get your degree? A baking school? Where are you cooking up these numbers?

Ron Blackwell: Oh that's an insult. You're a joker. You're an asshole.[5]

---

personal level, Olbermann is also apparently irascible, hypercontrolling, and generally not a team player. He, for instance, refused to share the spotlight on Current TV. See Brian Stelter, "Olbermann in a Clash at New Job," January 4, 2012, www.nytimes.com/2012/01/05/business/media/olbermann-in-a-clash-at-new-job.html?_r=1.

5. Sam Stein, "Neil Cavuto Called an 'Asshole' by AFL-CIO Economist on Live TV," *Huffington Post,* June 25, 2010, with video, www.huffingtonpost.com/2010/06/25/neil-cavuto-called-an-ass_n_626211.html.

Blackwell apparently felt it was not sufficient to call Cavuto a "joker." Cavuto was not trying to be funny, nor is he dull or uninformed and pretending to be otherwise. Cavuto fully grasps the difference between job creation and *net* job creation, and he knew full well what point Blackwell was making. He therefore cannot be classified as a mere "ass," with the suggestion of donkeylike stubbornness of mind combined with obliviousness to basic concepts or the social situation. Cavuto in fact staged a ploy: a dodge. He shifted attention away from the point made to the qualifications of the person making it in order to score dialectical points with the audience.

This is at the very least an asshole move. One often can permissibly shift attention in a conversation, but here it is at best unclearly justified. Interrupting Blackwell several times and then accusing him of not answering his question does not count as even half-cooperative discourse, not even by the low standards of American politics. Even that would not have been so bad if Cavuto had meant to initiate something like a meta-conversation between the two speakers, a conversation in which Blackwell could have later complimented the tactic of diversion with a "touché!" or "well played, sir." Cavuto betrays no hint of metacooperation. He simply feels entitled not to wait his conversational turn. He does not have to actually *listen* to an opposing perspective, even from the person he is talking to. Cavuto could perhaps argue that the host must exert heavy control over the terms of debate, because polite terms will not do. Or maybe he feels justified in his bullying as long as he is scoring points in a kind of televised game show, with influence, profit, and fun as his justly deserved reward. Either rationale could constitute a sense of entitlement—something like the right to rule, or at least to shut the opposition out, while taking the moral high ground.

Bill O'Reilly is the original cable news asshole and among the founding Uncompromising Arbiters of Real American Values Who Heroically Fight Corrupt Liberals as a Moral Bulwark Against the Decline of Civilization. So it is interesting to observe that O'Reilly has become less of an asshole in recent years. Why is unclear. He enjoyed marked success as a politico-asshole entrepreneur. But with others flooding into a new, well-rewarded role, perhaps he was out-assholed on both the political left and right. What to do then? Out-asshole the out-assholers? Perhaps O'Reilly didn't have it in him. Perhaps this just seemed unappealing or lowly. Perhaps he was admirably tempered by an authentic need to be, or at least be seen as, the Reasonable Common Man. If so, this is laudable and good, and it takes some of the edge off watching him. It even encourages appreciation for his mastery and formidable display of the dark asshole arts in verbal debate: the selective outrage, marshaled in defense of the victimized common man; the dogged quibbles over petty details; the seizing of any interlocutory moment of weakness (such as a pause for thought); the refusal to see and understand, supposedly on righteous principle but mainly to distort and distract.[6] One would almost admire his scrappy tenacity were he a real underdog rather than a very rich and extremely influential member of the political elite. (The real victimized common man has stagnating wages and uncertain work, perhaps a TV but not his own show on TV.)

It is not just Fox News commentators but Fox News itself that has the appropriate, in-your-face, I'm-entitled-to-do-this,

6. Thus David Letterman cleverly spoke for the common man (or at least the registered Democrats) in an exchange with O'Reilly over comments made about the Iraq war: "I'm not smart enough to debate you point to point on this, but I have the feeling . . . about sixty percent of what you say is crap." http://newsbusters.org/media/2006-01-03-CBSLSDL.wmv.

especially-because-you-dislike-it vibe. Which should not be surprising from a tightly controlled outfit in which everything flows from a single source, chairman Roger Ailes.[7] Ailes has personal flaws that do not necessarily make one an asshole but that clearly shape the coverage, including his paranoia[8] and his extreme politics.[9] We find more telling evidence by considering the man in a happy moment, a victory lap. In an event celebrating Fox News's success, Ailes said of the competing networks' talent, as though sharing in the agony of their defeat: "Shows, stars, I mean it's sad, you know? . . . I called and asked them all to move to the second floor wherever they were working. Because when they jump, I don't want it to hurt."[10] By which he meant that he wouldn't mind at all if his competitors not only

---

7. A former executive with Fox News's parent, News Corp., suggests a culture of intimidation. "It's like the Soviet Union or China: People are always looking over their shoulders. . . . There are people who turn people in." Rush Limbaugh, a friend, explains the centrality of Ailes personality: "One man has established a culture for 1,700 people who believe in it, who follow it, who execute it. . . . Roger Ailes does not ever show up on camera. And yet everybody who does is a reflection of him." Tim Dickinson, "How Roger Ailes Built the Fox News Fear Factory," *Rolling Stone,* May 25, 2011, www.rollingstone .com/politics/news/how-roger-ailes-built-the-fox-news-fear-factory-20110525. Unless otherwise noted, the factual assertions about Ailes in the text below are corroborated in detail in this article.

8. Ailes has an elaborate security detail and constant anxiety of personally being subject to an al-Qaeda terrorist attack. One false alarm with a dark-skinned man led him to order a lockdown of the Fox News building. The man was a janitor.

9. Rupert Murdoch, head of Fox's parent company, News Corp., reportedly says of his extremist politics: "You know Roger is crazy. He really believes that stuff." Dickinson, "How Roger Ailes Built the Fox News Fear Factory."

10. Brian Stelter, "Victory Lap for Fox and Hannity," *New York Times,* October 9, 2011, www.nytimes.com/2011/10/10/business/media/fox-news-and -hannity-at-the-top-after-15-years.html?_r=1&scp=2&sq=ailes&st=cse.

lost the contest but felt humiliated enough to kill themselves. He meant of course to gloat but also to show his contempt. He meant to *broadcast* his contempt and to have a laugh about his being in a position to advertise it.

The comment was at least poor sportsmanship. A longtime practitioner of blood sport media politics, Ailes has emerged as its undisputed heavyweight champion. Politics is indeed a rough sport, but there are still boundaries that while crossed are nevertheless there, or sort of there. It is possible to have a minimal sense of respect among fellow sportsmen, seen as equals off the playing field, and even to display grace in both victory and defeat. Ailes's comment suggests that he makes little effort at this, even as he does make an effort to draw attention to the fact that he cares not. He keeps it personal, on and off the court.

Ailes is a poor sport but not in a set contest fairly won. His main victory was to redefine the whole sport itself—that is to say, to redefine news. While American TV journalism has always walked a fine line between informing the public and satisfying media capitalism's demands for viewers, ratings, and ad dollars, the line was more or less there, and it represented respect for what some regard as the fourth branch of government and a democratic society that depends on real news. Ailes obliterates that line with his "orchestra pit theory," which he puts as follows: "If you have two guys on a stage and one guy says, 'I have a solution to the Middle East problem,' and the other guy falls in the orchestra pit, who do you think is going to be on the evening news?" The implication of course being that TV can and *should* cover the sensation rather than the substance, that it should move still *further* away from professional journalism and toward infotainment in a pure ratings contest. Fox News has changed the game and won, with an ever-thinner pretext of service. (It has very little actual news gathering and reporting staff; it freely crosses its own purported division between reporting and editorializing; and it now boosts for and even instigates protest movements and financially backs specific political candidates.) For its loyalty and attunement to its fans, it has been richly rewarded with outsized profits and unprecedented political influence.

If we ask why Ailes fought so long and so hard for all this, however, the answer is not simply the ample rewards. His victory lap comment also suggests fundamental contempt. It suggests contempt not just for his competitors but for a society of people who have always counted on news with a lot of information shaped by a good-faith attempt at impartial presentation. Our fundamental need in a democratic society, for each of us to make up our own mind, now goes unmet by the whole media environment. It reflects not the minds of equals deliberating together about what together to do but the tenor and voice of a single asshole's mind.

DELUSIONAL ASSHOLE

Cable news assholes are distinctive for their knowing awareness but willful disregard of how they are perceived by others. They are flush with Frankfurtian "bullshit," where bullshitting (speaking without regard for the truth) is something that can be done with a tacit understanding among speaker and audience that truth is not being told.[11] A quite different class of asshole,

11. Harry G. Frankfurt, *On Bullshit* (Princeton, NJ: Princeton University Press, 2005).

by contrast, is marked by his utter failure to appreciate how he is seen.

Such was the display in Paris at the fashion show debacle wrought by Kanye West's rough transition from pop music performer and producer to clothes designer. West had promised, with his fashion debut, to "change the course of fashion." When ill-fitting dresses, pants, and jackets, styled with bits of fur, were not well received, West complained bitterly, but not simply out of rudeness. As one reviewer explains:

> What was most confounding about Mr. West's behavior, after years of obsessive study of the industry, was that he demonstrated very little understanding of how he might actually be perceived by retailers and editors who have a vast amount of experience at detecting utter nonsense.[12]

West is not exactly shameless, which would require his having a clear sense of how others regard him. He is interesting more because he seems unable to piece that regard together, even from readily available material. Nor is it that he lacks a basic human capacity of self-observation, caused by some cognitive malfunction. His album *Graduation* begins "Mr. Fresh, Mr. . . . by his self he's so impressed," and the track "Barry Bonds" shows some grasp of how this must look to others: "I'm high up on the line you can get behind me / But my head so big you

12. Eric Wilson, "Kanye West, Designer (Yawn)," *New York Times,* October 5, 2011, www.nytimes.com/2011/10/06/fashion/kanye-west-designer-yawn .html?_r=1&adxnnl=1&ref=ericwilson&adxnnlx=1317923369-PMvObE5LY vsSTzJYBKN24A.

can't sit behind me."[13] But beyond general impressions, and his awareness of obvious sneers (he complained in Paris that the fashionistas keep looking at him "like I'm Hitler"), West seems unable to pick up his reflection in the eyes of others, from what is evident to all. Would fur in the summertime really be the Second Coming in the fashion world? Was it *unthinkable* that people would question that as a design idea?

West is also awfully rude (he constantly swears, and famously crashed Taylor Swift's MTV award acceptance speech, insulting Swift to boot). And of course many a self-styled, self-described genius has lived in massive error about his greatness. West is of special interest because he seems almost unable to move from huge self-absorption to a rudimentary grasp of the public world.[14] He probably *is* able, and so we recoil from his failure to treat others decently. But the sense of inability is enough to turn pure revulsion into mixed sympathy. For all we really know, we, too, could be a brain in a vat, or subsisting on an experience machine, or living inside the Matrix. (How would you know otherwise?) It is hard to watch someone who is in effect living that out, someone who *is* trapped in a giant delusion.

---

13. Jon Pareles, "The Ego Sessions: Will Success Spoil Kanye West," *New York Times,* September 5, 2007, www.nytimes.com/2007/09/05/arts/music/05west .html?ref=kanyewest, offers these lyrics as evidence of West's self-awareness, even suggesting the distinctive, West-inspired name "starcissism," for "a pop star's mixture of self-love, self-promotion, self-absorption and self-awareness." Pareles wrote before the Paris fashion debacle, when the suggestion was more plausible.

14. It is not easy, after all, living with a profound sense of divine purpose. As West explains, "God chose me. He made a path for me. . . . I am God's vessel." Except that his greatest worry is not letting God down. As he goes on to explain, "But my greatest pain in life is that I will never be able to see myself perform live." See "Kanye: 'I Am God's Vessel,'" www.metro.co.uk/metrolife/ 565894-kanye-i-am-gods-vessel.

It is instructive to compare West to asshole artists such as Pablo Picasso or Ernest Hemingway or Miles Davis. None were mistaken about their greatness. All were wrong about what their greatness entitled them to by way of special treatment from others.[15] Here it is harder to be understanding. It is indeed desirable for a society to afford its great artists special opportunities for creative production for the good of all. But there are limits, and many true geniuses do manage well enough to abide by them, perhaps by nurturing a grounding sense of gratitude for being endowed with special creative privilege. Those who don't are pure asshole. They take full credit for their achievements and expect further benefits in return, despite the fact that their success would never have happened without society's gift of creative opportunity. (Artists who must fend for food or fight against an invading army tend not to get a lot of art done.) Things could easily have gone differently and the artist would never have succeeded. Gauguin, for example, might have never made it to Tahiti if the boat from France had encountered bad weather or mechanical troubles, much as many great talents fail simply because they are ahead of their time. We put up with the artist's delusion that his work is only to *his* credit, that it is *we* who are chiefly in his debt, because we find our world better with his artworks in it. Without that, however, the asshole artist becomes thoroughly repugnant. Imagine a *failed* artist who is not a genius, who continually demands further creative privilege, perhaps at a significant cost to society, and who cannot be

---

15. A particularly stark example is Buddy Rich, whose greatness as a drummer is nearly matched by his rudeness, justified in the name of his own artistic perfection. Observe his rancid eloquence in addressing those not quite up to snuff at www.youtube.com/watch?v=q-ssZeOZkWU.

moved by or even grasp gentle advice that he should consider working at Starbucks, where people are actually served. This guy, we want to say, is an asshole in spades.[16]

THE DELUSIONAL ASSHOLE BANKER

Artists are of course usually more prone to self-loathing than to delusions of grandeur. The same cannot be said of bankers of late. Bankers, as a culture, have an extraordinary sense of their own importance with a correspondingly extraordinary sense of entitlement to monetary reward. This amounts to a grand delusion, which the recent global financial crisis has helped almost everyone except bankers to see through. Bankers sit somewhere in between West and Picasso: not entirely delusional about their importance but wildly delusional about what that importance means.

To see this, we should rehearse some properly uncontroversial truths. Financial markets do indeed have an essential func-

16. It is still important that we feel different about the successful artist such as Gauguin. In "Moral Luck," Bernard Williams argues that Gauguin's success in Tahiti substantively mitigates our moral feelings about his having abandoned his family in France for a risky artistic venture. See *Moral Luck: Philosophical Papers, 1973–1980* (Cambridge: Cambridge University Press, 1981), 23–26. Gauguin might thus seem less of an asshole than he would have been had he never made it to Tahiti, or never found inspiration, even if this resulted simply from a stroke of bad luck that reflected nothing about him or his character. But we might also say that he is equally an asshole whether he succeeded or failed. As Thomas Nagel explains, our specifically moral objection to Gauguin might consider only the choices he made when his artistic prospects were uncertain. ("Moral Luck," in *Mortal Questions* (Cambridge: Cambridge University Press, 1979), 24–38. Is this *ex ante* perspective the right one for assessing someone as an asshole? Or should we also look at who the person actually perchance becomes over time, including any ultimate contribution to human culture? We leave this deep problem unresolved.

tion in a capitalist society. A capitalist society's guiding idea is precisely that a society will put its savings to its most productive uses, for the sake of an overall improvement in living standards, by allowing resources to be allocated by financial markets rather than centralized decisions. The goal is not freedom per se. It is not enough that traders are left free to transact (and so pool information, spread risk, and so on). If the basic purpose of financial markets is to be served, the functioning system has to *actually lead to improved living standards by boosting production in the real economy.* This by no means happens automatically. World history is replete with financial crises that did lasting and catastrophic damage to whole economies (e.g., the Great Depression, the "lost decades" in Argentina or Japan) and to people's whole lives (e.g., people lost their homes, retirees lost much of their savings, eager workers were left unemployed, college graduates saw worse employment prospects over the longer haul, and so on).[17] In recent decades, after many insisted that "this time is different," because the risks of crises have been reduced, the 2008–9 financial crisis and ensuing Great Recession made it abundantly plain that painful crises can and will continue to break out. Few issues compare in importance with whether financial markets function in the right way, such that their basic function in a capitalist economy is well served.

To continue with basic truths: with the United States, where the crisis first broke, as an example, the economy saw its greatest rise in general prosperity during the "boring" postwar years, before financial "innovation," when the "best and brightest" did other things, largely of a scientific or engineering nature.

17. Carmen M. Reinhardt and Kenneth S. Rogoff, *This Time Is Different: Eight Centuries of Financial Folly* (Princeton, NJ: Princeton University Press, 2009). part 5.

A key cause of the recent crisis (among many causes) was that, through mathematically sophisticated "innovation," firms and traders were allowed to take on far too much risk. Once it became clear that the prices of fiercely complex financial instruments had little connection with the real value of real assets (e.g., homes), the whole system unraveled. The markets have continued to function only because large firms were bailed out by governments, with taxpayers picking up the tab. With little choice in the moment of crisis, society in effect assumes the risk so that firms and traders can continue to reap huge rewards.

We consider how this might reflect a larger culture of entitlement in chapter 7. For now, let us focus on particular people and, in particular, an unusually candid conversation among two bankers and two journalists in a Wall Street bar. The journalists are suggesting that the bankers should be grateful to society that it bailed out their industry and saved their jobs. The bankers disagree, arguing that their jobs are to their own credit and, in particular, their smartness.

> Jane Feltes: You think you got to keep your job because you're smart? You got to keep your job because you guys got bailed out. You guys got bailed—
> Bar Patron 2: No, no, no, no, no. That's not what happened with my job. I mean, survival of the fittest.
> Bar Patron 1: Because I'm smarter than the average person.
> Davidson: And even if the government bails out your industry that failed, you still say it's because you're smarter.
> Bar Patron 1: No. The government bailing out an industry was out of necessity for whatever the situation

was. The fact that I benefited from that is because
I'm smart. I took advantage of a situation. Ninety-five
percent of the population doesn't have that common
sense. The only reason I've been doing this for so
long is because I must be smarter than the next guy.

Bar Patron 1 credits his job *entirely to his own talent.* Notice
that he does not deny the plain fact that society has just bailed
out the whole industry, saving many "smart" people from
together wrecking the whole system. What he claims is that
this plain fact is nevertheless wholly *irrelevant* to what bankers
are due. The feeling seems to be widely shared in the industry.
Bankers feel very sure of their entitlement to enormous benefits,
and therefore feel mystified and even victimized by the suggestion that they are overpaid. Indeed, in interviews with bankers
about the Occupy Wall Street protesters, bankers privately say
that their critics lack an appropriate sense of gratitude.[18]

To say that this point of view is a massive delusion is of course
to assume that there are good reasons, available to all, for taking
the facts of the matter to be otherwise. There are many widely
cited reasons for this. There is, for example, the sheer enormity
of social costs of the crisis: by some estimates, enough to put
the banking industry out of business if it was actually asked

18. Nelson D. Schwartz and Eric Dash, "In Private, Wall St. Bankers Dismiss Protesters as Unsophisticated," *New York Times,* October 14, 2011,
www.nytimes.com/2011/10/15/business/in-private-conversation-wall-street
-is-more-critical-of-protesters.html?_r=1&ref=occupywallstreet. One banker
does argue that bankers contribute a lot in taxes. But of course the basic issue
is why bankers should have incomes high enough such that they pay a lot in
taxes.

to pay for the damage done.[19] There is the implicit government subsidy, which allows "too big to fail" banks to take ever-greater risks, knowing that they'll be bailed out if things go too far south, allowing bankers to take huge profits while taxpayers assume the risks.[20] And, if nothing else, there is the fact that the run-up to the recent crisis involved fraud on a massive scale, which has largely been left unpunished, with profits intact. With some exceptions, few have paid for breaking the law.

Why do these reasons fail to move general banker opinion? Bar Patron 1 might simply be reasoning as a psychopath: he's not using moral concepts like *deserts* or *gratitude* but simply reporting what happened—the government bailed out the industry—and then reporting that he has in any case, in the "survival-of-the-fittest" manner, profited as a result of his smarts. That is no reason, however, to think that he *shouldn't* feel grateful for having his industry bailed out, for being able to keep his well-paid job. Yet Bar Patron 1 seems to be saying precisely that he *owes no debt of gratitude,* a clear *moral* claim. In that case, his reasoning is better put as follows: he deserves his rewards, because our system reliably and justly rewards talent, and because he is especially smart. He *must* be smart, because he is in fact well paid, and because *our system is in fact the kind of system that reliably metes out just deserts.*

This thesis is of course pretty rich in light of the fact that our current system has just done inordinate damage to the real

19. According to the Bank of England's Andrew G. Haldane in "The $100 Billion Question," a lecture available at www.bis.org/review/r100406d.pdf.
20. Former IMF head Simon Johnson and James Kwak argue for breaking up the big banks on these grounds in *13 Bankers: The Wall Street Takeover and the Next Financial Meltdown* (New York: Pantheon, 2010).

economy (unless of course the system is reliably rewarding the talent for doing inordinate damage). But let us assume that Bar Patron 1's perspective is grounded more in a philosophical outlook than in facts. Bar Patron 1 seems moved not by facts but by a certain *idea* of a capitalist society, the idea that, in a free market, people get what they deserve.

Even on philosophical grounds, however, this view is exceedingly hard to defend. That is true according to none other than the archconservative twentieth-century apologist for capitalism, F. A. Hayek. He writes:

> There is little a man can do to alter the fact that his special talents are very common or exceedingly rare. A good mind or a fine voice, a beautiful face or a skilful hand, a ready wit or an attractive personality are in a large measure as independent of a person's efforts as the opportunities or the experiences he has had. In all these instances the value which a person's capacities or services have for us and for which he is recompensed has little relation to anything that we can call moral merit or "deserts."[21]

The billionaire investor and oracular philosopher Warren Buffett echoes the point:

> My luck was accentuated by my living in a market system that sometimes produces distorted results, though overall it serves our country well. I've worked in an economy that rewards someone who saves the lives of others on a battle-

21. F. A. Hayek, *The Constitution of Liberty* (1960; repr., Chicago: University of Chicago Press, 2011), 158.

field with a medal, rewards a great teacher with thank-you notes from parents, but rewards those who can detect the mispricing of securities with sums reaching into the billions. In short, fate's distribution of long straws is wildly capricious.[22]

In other words, ideas of deserts just don't justify the going rate of rewards. Bar Patron 1 cannot infer his IQ or his deservingness from his paycheck.

Some bankers inadvertently confirm the point by offering plainly bad arguments in place of the appeal to deserts. Some argue, for example, that bankers should be appreciated because, as one money manager put it, "Financial services are one of the last things we do in this country and do it well. Let's embrace it."[23] This, again, is not exactly credible after the banking sector has just caused the largest crisis in seventy years. In any case, the financialization of the economy is less a matter of inherent skill than decades of political decisions that in effect passed up opportunities to invest in infrastructure and education that might have supported high-skilled manufacturing. Globalization might then have had a chance of bringing rising wages instead of a three-decade period in which increasingly productive workers have in effect not seen a pay raise.

Given the thinness of the arguments,[24] the honest bankers

22. Letter to *Fortune,* June 16, 2010, http://money.cnn.com/2010/06/15/news/newsmakers/Warren_Buffett_Pledge_Letter.fortune/index.htm.
23. Schwartz and Dash, "In Private, Wall St. Bankers Dismiss Protesters as Unsophisticated."
24. For present purposes I am assuming that the arguments against taking aggressive measures to stop crises are thin. I offer a more developed defense of that proposition in *Fairness in Practice: A Social Contract for a Global Economy* (New York: Oxford University Press, 2012), chap. 8.

are perhaps those who resort to cosmic grandiosity. Thus Lloyd C. Blankfein, head of Goldman Sachs, quips—with a definite whiff of Rockefeller or Beveridge or Rhodes—that bankers are "doing God's work." Blankfein may not be an asshole,[25] but this is an asshole remark, even if it was mildly ironic. It implies not *just* that bankers are "doing good things" but that their work is somehow within God's plan or somehow brings them closer to God. Even if the comment was merely a joke, it was a "fuck you" type of joke, given that it was made in public in the wake of a crisis that had just upended millions of lives. It suggests complete obliviousness to how others will hear the remark, though not simple cluelessness. The man is hardly an idiot, and so his obliviousness is better seen as expressing a sense of entitlement, in this case, apparently of an unspecified God-sized kind.

This attitude among the new bankers stands in marked contrast with bankers of an earlier era. Consider the former Goldman CEO John Whitehead, a member of the civic-minded "Greatest Generation" that ably steered the dynastic wealth of Rockefeller and the like toward the social good. In lamenting that executive compensation today discourages the long view, and so has "got to be changed," he explains why Blankfein, and by implication the new generation, "doesn't get it."

> [Blankfein] never thought that if the public is losing their jobs and we're in a recession, it isn't a very good time to talk about the justification for a $60 million bonus. He doesn't get it! . . . He says, "I'm the CEO of the best

---

25. Ron Suskind, *Confidence Men: Wall Street, Washington, and the Education of a President* (New York: HarperCollins, 2011), 424, describes Blankfein as "whipsawed between cocky and penitent." Penitence is usually a sign of not being an asshole. If he is an asshole, he's a half-ass asshole.

financial service firm in the world. And I'm the CEO, I'm its head man. I deserve to be paid more than anybody else. And I'm prepared to fight for it, and boast about it. Because I'm proud of it."[26]

But, much as with Bar Patron 1, Blankfein's appeal to deserts rings hollow in an industry that almost drove the global economy off a cliff.

We might put the general lesson this way: the banker's position of high reward is a *privilege*. The position itself exists only because of societal need and design. That any particular banker holds a given position is in large measure good luck. Since many people are hardworking enough and smart enough to do the job (again, financial markets worked better from a crisis-avoidance point of view before they became mathematically sophisticated), any given banker is replaceable: it would be equally well for society, or indeed better, if someone else took his or her place, *especially* if he or she is very talented, since talent is more important in medicine, teaching, or science. For those who do work in finance, the enormous benefits are a societal gift but with conditions attached. The financial system needs to be organized so that it reliably works to the benefit of real people in the real economy. When this requires significant reorganization—including such things as reserves requirements, international securities taxes, the segregation of investment and finance, expansion of IMF and ECB last-resort lending capacity, breaking up "too big to fail" banks—then bankers have no reasonable complaint. If a given banker doesn't like the gift, he or she can give it back (and seek work at Starbucks, a good high school, or a biology lab).

26. Suskind, *Confidence Men,* 425.

The banker's sense of special entitlement is therefore akin to that of our imagined failed asshole artist. Neither the banker nor the failed artist has produced the goods, and yet both go on complaining about not getting what they deserve, seemingly unable to grasp how this could be a colossal, delusional mistake.[27]

This hardly means that all or even most bankers are delusional assholes; some genuinely do understand why the public would be enraged. Carmine Visone, an older-school Lehman Brothers managing director, could never believe his social worth was what he was being paid and so served the homeless out of gratitude and responsibility to society.[28] Still, a delusional banking culture makes being an asshole especially easy, which may itself explain why asshole bankers seem in abundance lately.

27. Robert Nozick, the most famous philosophical libertarian, would defend banker pay not as a just deserts but as a matter of one's natural right to exchange with others without interference, in this case, in labor markets. See *Anarchy, State, and Utopia* (New York: Basic Books, 1974). Nozick admitted that such rights don't allow one to harm others, however, so one wouldn't have the right to create systemic risks that cause financial crises without also having to compensate those injured. Paying for the costs of crises may require dramatically scaling back financial markets with taxes that "make bankers pay." In addition, Nozick allows only a minimal state, whereas large-scale financial markets arguably depend on robust enabling institutions supported by taxation that Nozick would regard as theft. In a Nozickian paradise, large-scale financial markets arguably wouldn't exist.

28. Suskind, *Confidence Men,* 54.

[4] GENDER, NATURE, BLAME

❡ Having now examined numerous assholes, we observe a pattern: assholes are mainly men. Why should that be so? What explains why assholes are so overwhelmingly distributed among only one-half of the human population?

Is it because men have been socialized so differently from women—that is, is it a product of *culture*? Or is it something about men themselves—something about *male nature*—that explains why newborn boys are so much more likely to become assholes than are newborn girls?

The answer, we will suggest, is gender culture rather than maleness. Maleness per se, seen as a mere biological category, is not causally to blame, or at least any influence it has is swamped by deeply entrenched, nearly universal gender culture. This causal thesis implies nothing about morality by itself. It does raise a deep philosophical question about moral responsibility, about who, if anyone, is morally responsible for what. If culture systematically steers newborn babies into becoming assholes simply because their sex is male, how can the grown-up asshole be blamed or condemned for his foul condition? Responsibility might seem to lie squarely upon *society*. It allows gender culture to have this profoundly influential steering role. The foulness of the asshole may therefore seem to reflect not the foulness of the individuals we routinely blame for their asshole ways but rather the foulness of a social condition that produces assholes in abundance. We usually do single out the individual asshole, blaming *him*. But why should this be fair? Why isn't the lone asshole just a hapless soul caught up in a grand cultural asshole-production machine?

A measure of sympathy for an asshole might be laudable, but it shouldn't be taken too far. He still has freedom of will. He usually acts in his assholish ways freely and of his own free will. That is the source of his actions and the proper target for management, criticism, and blame—or so we want to maintain.

Philosophy won't simply take that for granted. The philosophical skeptic will deny it outright: according to the skeptic, no one, not even an asshole, is the appropriate object of condemnation or blame. Moral responsibility is, at most, a useful fiction. As usual in philosophy, there is no easy refutation of the dug-in skeptic. But even if refutation isn't in the cards, the skeptic's salutary role is to force those of us who aren't skeptical to *say* what we might mean in claiming that people do indeed have "freedom of will." Why is it, exactly, that assholes are the appropriate object of blame, whereas the insane or the drug addict are not justly held responsible? What, precisely, is the difference?

In one traditional interpretation, the asshole indeed has freedom of will, and so qualifies for blame, in the sense that he has *control* over his actions and the nature of his character. His actions and character are finally up to him, despite the strong cultural currents he swims in. As we will see, however, requiring this special kind of countercultural control makes blaming the asshole more problematic than it needs to be. There is a better, more modest interpretation of what his freedom of will consists of that more easily saddles him with moral responsibility. Roughly, the asshole is rightly to blame simply because of the outlook reflected in his behavior, simply because he thinks like an asshole in a way that makes his actions his own. That is true whether or not he is "free" in any further way and whether or not he has any further special control over his fate in the cultural asshole-production machine. He can be a product of the machine and blameworthy anyway.

ASSHOLES AND BACHELORS

Before we delve further, we should consider the possibility that our supposedly profound philosophical questions are founded upon a huge but simple mistake. It is not quite true, we might say, that assholes are *mainly* men. Rather, assholes are *only* men, and for a simple and completely unmysterious purely *linguistic* reason: the term "asshole" refers only to men *by definition,* in just the way the term "bachelor" refers only to unmarried men. We simply agree, by linguistic convention, to use the term "asshole" in a gendered way, much as we do with "bastard." We could have equally coordinated speech behavior in a different way. And, it may be suggested, we do indeed have a useful further name for the same kind of person when that person happens to be female: we call her a "bitch." If this is right, there is no grand mystery about why assholes are men: this reflects nothing more than the way we happen to use words.

Natural as it might seem, this view is wrong. Suppose I consider the proposition that Ann Coulter is an asshole. I don't feel forced to withhold that term simply because she is not a man. Rather, there is a *substantive debate* to have about whether she qualifies (or rather how she could fail to qualify) as an asshole. That debate cannot be settled by reflecting on how we happen to use words. If I ask instead whether Coulter is a "bachelor," the question is plainly confused. A bachelor is by definition an unmarried *man* (of a certain age, etc.), much in the way a spinster is by definition a woman. That holds simply because of how we use words. "Female bachelor" is a contradiction in terms. "Female asshole" is an interesting possibility (and, I would say, a reality in cases like Coulter).

To take a more complicated example, the suggestion that "Tiger Mom" Amy Chua is an asshole isn't undermined by the mere fact that she is a woman. There's a case to make that she is an asshole, but it won't suffice simply to observe her tough parenting methods, which have included calling her daughter Lulu "garbage" in order to motivate her; rejecting a birthday card because "I deserve better than this"; and turning her house into a "war zone" in order to coerce Lulu into learning a difficult piano piece, despite objections from her husband that she was insulting her by calling her "lazy, cowardly, self-indulgent and pathetic."[1] One can be a misguidedly tough parent without being an asshole, perhaps by standing ready to reconsider one's parental prerogatives, including one's assumptions about what is best for one's children. What set Chua apart was that she wrote with maternal bravado, certitude, and claim to superiority, all based on the questionable assumption that child achievement is all important, while inviting suspicion that she's concerned as much with her own status in light of her daughters' success or failure as with their health and happiness. On the other hand, she is in fact deeply concerned for the welfare of her daughters, sincere and articulate in her views, and open to changing her

---

1. "Why Chinese Mothers Are Superior," *Wall Street Journal,* January 8, 2001, http://online.wsj.com/article/SB10001424052748704111504576059713528698 754.html, and Amy Chua, *Battle Hymn of the Tiger Mother* (New York: Penguin Press, 2011).

mind.[2] She has in fact softened her views and manner, showing that she is not entrenched in the way assholes are. (Coulter, by contrast, shows no sign of easing up.) Chua is ultimately not an asshole, but, again, her gender is quite beside the point.

If women can be assholes, the fact that assholes are mainly men presents a deep explanatory problem. Things presumably could have been otherwise. In a fairer world, assholes might be distributed equally across the male and female human population, giving newborn males and newborn females roughly equal chances of becoming or not becoming assholes. Given that things are as they are, however, we have to ask why the asshole type crops up in the set of human beings born male so much more often than the set of human beings born female. This is a truly marvelous fact of life, which presumably has some explanation. But what?

THE BITCH

A natural answer is: pervasive gender roles. To appreciate how powerful this is as a potential explanation, consider the following definition of "bitch," which shadows our definition of "asshole." A person counts as a *bitch,* we may say, when, and only when, she systematically takes special advantages in interpersonal relations out of an entrenched sense of entitlement that *leaves her open to the voiced or expressed complaints of other people, but immunized against their motivational influence.*

---

2. And in any case she quite rightly takes objection to recent, approval-obsessed Western styles of parenting, which have made kids tend toward either self-destructive anxiety or narcissism and the desperate need to experience something real (e.g., through college binge-drinking experiences).

The only difference between the asshole and the bitch, in this proposal, appears in the italicized phrase "leaves her open to the voiced or expressed complaints of other people, but immunized against their motivational influence." In other words, the bitch *listens* to the voiced complaints of others, making at least a *show* of recognition. Nevertheless, what is said makes no motivational difference to what she does; once her face-to-face encounter with you is over, it is as though you never talked. She "recognizes" you in one sense: she acts as though she feels it is important to hear you out, to entertain your concerns. But this turns out to be only for show. In her private reasoning and motivation, she is, in the end, insusceptible to anything you might have said. Her sense of entitlement is "entrenched," in that sense, but not so entrenched that she is unwilling even to entertain voiced complaints. The bitch betrays you behind your back. The asshole fails to recognize you to your face.

One advantage to the asshole is that his ugly conduct takes place out in the open. This makes him easier to avoid. The bitch presents uncertainty, because hidden motives are harder to discern. Some bitches may not be particularly good at feigning concern face-to-face. Other bitches are convincing. You really feel things have been sorted out between you, and that you really are mutually understanding and responsive to each other's concerns, until you later learn that the discussion made no difference. Perhaps you learn this by happenstance, only after seeing how things play out, perhaps over numerous similar occasions, after repeatedly giving the benefit of the doubt and being let down.

On the other hand, assholes are especially outrageous in a crucial way: they don't even offer a *show* of respect. A show of respect is, after all, a *form of respect,* however unsatisfactory. We don't make a show of respect to a fence post, since it isn't the kind of thing to which respect is even in principle owed. With people, by contrast, showing respect is all important for good relationships, whether in international diplomacy, life in the workplace, or friendship and intimate relationships.

The bitch fully appreciates all this. In that sense she does recognize persons as moral equals, albeit in a circumstantial way. The asshole is especially outrageous because, whatever his private motives, *he can't even be polite.* And even when he is polite, or even charming, fundamental respect is not the reason why. Other motives are in play.

Now, if this is correct, we can explain why assholes are mainly men. Moreover, we don't have to assume anything special about the very nature of biological maleness. We look only to the powerful influence of gendered socialization. Men and women are raised very differently in most cultural settings. That difference in upbringing and social expectations is what does the work. For instance, males are generally taught to be assertive and outspoken, while females are taught to remain silent or pull their punches—and sharply sanctioned when they don't. In that case, even if males and females are equally disposed at birth to the required entrenched sense of entitlement, that sense might manifest itself and develop into very different behaviors and character traits in adulthood. Entitled women might find it relatively difficult to openly, brazenly shut others out, since such conduct is aggressively sanctioned in the social group. Men might find this relatively easy. In their case, people tend to look the other way ("Boys will be boys," they might say). They expect assertive behavior from men and boys and are not surprised that a few bad apples go too far with it. Assertive women and girls, by contrast, are considered way out of line.

We do sometimes say that someone is a "born asshole," suggesting that he came into his condition as early as birth. It could be, in theory, that some people are born with characteristics (e.g., high testosterone levels or a propensity to aggression or to social insensitivity) that predispose them, by nature, to become assholes later in life. Gender culture might simply channel these underlying natural dispositions (which may reflect an evolutionary history that is itself shaped by coevolving gender culture, creating a nature-culture "chicken-and-egg" problem). Still, nurture surely has *some* role in shaping which and how many such people actually flower into the assholes they become, and it is easy to believe that it has at least a *major* role in asshole development. A particularly strong counterasshole culture would presumably suppress inborn tendencies, even if it couldn't go so far as to turn every born son into a kindly fellow. If good society could have this dampening influence, it would seem that nurture, not nature, is doing the causal work when a society lets assholes run wild.

Gender theory largely concurs. Gender concepts of "male" and "female" are deeply socially constructed, and only *appear* natural.[3] Our various identities—whether "male," "female," or "none of the above"—are constructed through the "intersectionality" of political power, class, race, and history.[4] While much

3. As Simone de Beauvoir puts the point, "Social discriminations . . . produce in women moral and intellectual effects so profound that they appear to spring from her original nature." *The Second Sex* (1949; repr., Harmondsworth: Penguin, 1972), 18.
4. On the diversity of cultural influences, see Elizabeth V. Spelman, *Inessential Woman: Problems of Exclusion in Feminist Thought* (Boston: Beacon Press, 1988), and Patricia Hill Collins, *Black Feminist Thought: Knowledge, Consciousness, and the Politics of Empowerment* (New York: Routledge, 2000).

of this is culturally specific, gender categories are used almost everywhere to enforce patriarchy.[5]

In the present context, such feminist critiques come to the aid of maleness. It is not the maleness of males per se that explains the proliferation of masculine assholes. It is not that *men* are assholes, as though non-asshole men have somehow *overcome* their inherently male asshole tendencies. Rather, the influence of gender culture is just very deep. Deep gender culture, not maleness, is primarily to blame for the fact that assholes are mainly men.[6]

THE CULTURAL PRODUCTION OF ASSHOLES

Without pretending to settle the deep question of asshole causation, let us assume for the sake of argument that culture can make people into assholes. Since culture varies widely, we should expect this to work differently across different times and places (even if nearly universal patriarchy sets some general constraints). This in turn poses the question, Do some societies tend to produce assholes in larger numbers relative to the general population than other societies relative to theirs? Are there more assholes per capita in the United States than in Japan, or in Italy than in Finland? Or does every society have

5. For a Marxist take, see Maria Mies, *Patriarchy and Accumulation on a World Scale: Women in the International Division of Labour* (London: Zed Books, 1998).

6. According to Judith Butler, in *Gender Trouble: Feminism and the Subversion of Identity* (London: Routledge, 1999), however, even biological sex categories are socially constructed. As a component of socially constructed gender, "maleness" isn't off the causal hook, but rather not a distinct causal variable. Instead of coming to the aid of maleness, this view denies its existence as natural.

roughly the same percentage of assholes in its population and asshole behavior is merely expressed differently according to different prevailing social norms? If we answer that asshole to non-asshole ratios can vary from place to place, we might also wonder about change over time: Are there more assholes than there used to be in the United States as compared to a control group such as Canada, or in Brazil as compared to a control group such as Argentina or Peru?

The answer to all these questions is, It sure seems so, at least from the casual-traveler anthropologist's point of view. Not only do some societies, such as the United States or Italy or Brazil, seem to produce many more assholes than other societies, but each seems to have more assholes than it used to. Maybe societies such as South Africa have fewer assholes in the wake of the apartheid years. If we look at global trends, though, asshole production seems to be on the rise.

One could argue that asshole production proceeds at a uniform and steady rate and that there has merely been an increase in asshole *reporting,* with increasing media scrutiny of public figures and profit-driven exposure of assholes on TV, in print, and on the Web. At the same time, however, increasing reportage also *creates* powerful incentives for assholes to bare themselves in public, for a large audience. That could itself cause asshole production to rise on average.

Here much depends on how we should interpret cultural difference. We might recall cross-cultural variation in what counts as rude behavior, as in familiar East-West contrasts. This makes it hard to tell who is or who is not an asshole. Many Asian cultures regard loud talking in public as a mark of self-centeredness and attention seeking. The South Korean asshole who visits the United States, where self-expression rather than modesty is generally prized, would have to be especially loud to stand out. On the other hand, in a South Korean university, a visiting American student who is used to being encouraged to speak up in class could easily be mistaken for an asshole if he hadn't yet noticed that interrupting a professor in lecture is seen as disrespectful. The confusion can persist in perceptions of whole cultures. In a developing South Asian nation such as Indonesia, it is hard for the American or British traveler not to feel that the country is overrun with assholes, given that queuing at the airport (or on the airplane) seems so much like a scrum. It takes a while to see that there is in fact a semblance of order: one is to be as pushy as possible about relative line position without simply pushing others out of the way. (Indonesians don't share the American or British allergy to actually touching other people.) And there is no clear sign of asshole overproduction among the Indonesian people more generally. If anything, Indonesia underperforms in this way.

Given such cultural differences, one might be skeptical about whether there is any statistically significant cross-cultural or cross-temporal variation in how many assholes are getting produced. The issue is finally one for anthropologists and sociologists to settle. Still, to at least suggest why the steady state view might be wrong, why there might be real variation in asshole production, we might offer anecdotal evidence and a bit of theoretical speculation.

First the anecdotal evidence, from a kind of transnational association. Traveling Brazilian surfers, so almost everyone agrees, are much more likely to be assholes than surfers from almost anywhere else. Acting like an asshole is plainly encouraged in the subculture of Brazilian surfers, who tend to travel in large packs (e.g., of five or ten people as compared to the usual one or two or three). This probably reflects the aggressive manliness of larger Brazilian culture but also has a more salient and direct explanation in the relatively recent past. When Brazilians first started showing up on Oahu's famous North Shore, they were antagonized by local Hawaiians, despite mainly lying low. Hawaiian surfers had already become defensive about white visiting surfers from California, Australia, and South Africa and were especially sore about the bombastic Aussies who began to dominate in surf contests and brag loudly about it. White surfers seemed to be continuing a neocolonial expropriation of the last thing the islanders had left—they at least still ruled the world-class surf breaks.[7] The brown-skinned Brazilians didn't quite fit into the "hoale" mold, coming a bit too close for comfort to the local style. But after many sound beatings and much damage to surfboards, Brazilians learned both to fight and to travel in large, protective groups. This worked well. So well that they now regularly take the same aggressive ethos to surf breaks around the world. They trash otherwise mellow and joyous surf lineups in Tahiti or Indonesia in any number of ways: they show up all at the same time, shifting the lineup into a hypercompetitive mode; they break or cheat the rules of position and right-of-way; they threaten to "take it to the beach" when complaints are made; and they do indeed get into a fair number of fights.

That is an example of how a culture can create assholes that might not otherwise exist. We can now offer a more theoretical speculation about how this could happen on a larger societal scale. Perhaps "collectivist" cultures are less likely to engender or tolerate the required sense of entitlement than are "individualist" ones. Consider some individualistic political philosophies. Whether widely avowed or simply in the air, some have a clear

7. The whole story is nicely documented in *Bustin' Down the Door,* www.imdb .com/title/tt1129921/.

entitlement message that may push many mere would-be assholes over the line. The would-be asshole might embrace the
philosophy he is already inclined toward and take succor in the
fact that some seemingly smart or respected people agree. That
may cement his self-confidence during his tender years, leaving
him with the easier task of noting how many fools fail to grasp
what any sufficiently intelligent and truly worthy person would
readily see. Yet were the very same child reared in a culture in
which deference and cooperation are seen as all-important, his
sense of entitlement would never have developed or been sup-
pressed, and he would never have become the asshole he now is.

So, for example, given that the United States seems to have
more than its share of assholes, it would be interesting to know
how many impressionable young Americans read Ayn Rand's
Objectivism-soaked novels and how those numbers compare
in Japan, where assholes seem comparatively rare. We might
also compare the effects of self-esteem-boosting parenting and
Internet social networking, which are increasingly making narcissism a sociocultural disease, and may explain the precipitous
drop in empathy among college students (especially after the
year 2000, after social networking caught on).[8] Without strong
collectivist counterpressures, it would be surprising *not* to see a
spike in the asshole population.

CAN ASSHOLES BE BLAMED?

Assholes, then, are made and not born. They are made by a society's gender culture. A newborn boy in the United States or Italy

8. This is according to a University of Michigan study, described in "Empathy:
College Students Don't Have as Much as They Used To," May 26, 2010, www
.newswise.com/articles/view/565005/?sc=lwtr;xy=5017391.

or Israel is much more likely to live the life of an asshole than a newborn boy in Japan or Norway or Canada. This brings us back to the disquieting possibility that assholes are morally not to blame for their condition. Responsibility for what the asshole does may lie with the culture that made him rather than with the asshole himself. Our discussion has been founded on the assumption that we rightly feel not simply bothered or annoyed but *indignant* or *resentful* about how the asshole treats us. It is now time to take seriously the possibility that this assumption is wrong. While the asshole of course makes a huge mess of things, it may well be that, ultimately, his hands are morally clean: he is foul but not to blame.

Why take this possibility seriously? Here is a serious philosophical argument for the skeptical view that assholes are not morally responsible. According to the argument, reactions of indignation, resentment, or any other form of blame will be appropriate only if the asshole is responsible for what he does. More specifically, the asshole will be responsible for what he does only if or to the extent that what he does is *fully within his control*. But, in general, the asshole is not fully in control of what he does. What he does simply reflects who he is, where who he is mainly reflects the culture into which he is born and raised; where that is, of course, is something over which he has little or no control. Hence, the asshole is not responsible for what he does and so is not the appropriate object of indignation, resentment, or any other form of blame.

The intuitive idea can be framed in terms of luck. Plenty of people manage not to become assholes. This is mainly good luck for them; it happens because of all kinds of factors that were beyond their control (e.g., being born into the right family). Likewise, anyone who becomes an asshole suffers a major stroke of bad luck, which could have easily gone the other way. A

given American asshole, say, would most likely not have become
an asshole had he been born and raised just across the border in
Canada. It is an unfortunate fact of life that he is an asshole, for
him and for us, but he can hardly be blamed for being born on
the wrong side of a border.

The problem becomes more difficult when we recall that
assholes rarely if ever fundamentally change. That is not to
say they *cannot* change—a few, after all, do see the moral
light. But it might seem unreasonable to *expect* them to change.
It might be that we should see being an asshole as a kind of
culturally induced mental handicap that society must simply
accommodate and accept. Indeed, if society is chiefly responsible for the asshole's plight, it may seem *especially* unfair that
it consigns so many people to a condition from which there
is only a slim chance of escape. The appropriate response
to the asshole is not then indignation or resentment but
sympathy—sympathy for a fellow person who is locked inside an
egocentric cage.

While sympathy is a good quality, this is hard to swallow. No
one, after all, is forcing the asshole to speak too loudly or abuse
his position of power. He does these things of his own free will,
of his own accord. Is he not then rightly to blame? Perhaps. But
the question then is what exactly this "freedom of will" consists
of. We haven't defended our right to place blame until we've said
what that could possibly mean.

Here, then, is one traditional answer: assholes do indeed
have full control over their actions, and they are properly
blamed for how they choose to exercise it. You are to blame for
killing someone with your car when you could have swerved
out of the way or could have had your brakes checked. You are
not to blame if the accident resulted from a car pileup that was

entirely out of your control. You had, or lacked, "full control" over those outcomes, in the sense required for you to count as morally responsible for them.

This view feels natural but also courts skepticism about moral responsibility in its own way. The assumption is still that the asshole is responsible for what he does *only if* what he does is fully in his control. But in what sense is anyone ever *fully* in control of what one does? The answer depends on what "fully" means. When the asshole speaks too loudly, he acts in character; he acts from the entrenched sense of entitlement that defines who he is. But, it may seem, the asshole is *fully* in control of his speaking too loudly only if he is *also* fully in control of his becoming that kind of person. Yet is any asshole really *fully in control of his having become an asshole*? Can we really say that every asshole we want to blame has somehow freely chosen his characterological fate from a position of full control over who he would finally become? This seems a stretch. Again, culture has a huge role. The cultural crosscurrents that drew a given asshole into his condition needn't have *determined* his fate in order to have deprived him of "full control" over who he has in fact become. He could have simply been going with the cultural flow like almost everyone else. Maybe he even shaped his own process of development. Still, that won't amount to his having had "full control" over the outcome. Who one becomes is generally not in one's control in the way it is in my control, say, whether or not I raise my arm (with no one holding it down, etc.).[9]

9. The foregoing is roughly a version of the skepticism defended by Galen Strawson in "The Impossibility of Moral Responsibility," *Philosophical Studies* 75 (1994): 5–24, if we substitute "full control" for a kind of conscious choosing (which he specifies).

To press the point, we can ask: When would this free choice from a position of full control supposedly have occurred? Many assholes are teenagers who never grew up. But a *teenager* can hardly be said to have at some point stepped out of his ego-centric predicament and cast a free vote in favor of staying or becoming an asshole instead of developing into a fully coopera-tive adult. More likely, the thought of doing things differently just didn't occur to him. He went in the direction of defensive-ness instead of personal growth mainly because this seemed to work out pretty well for him. He mostly got what he wanted out of this. Perhaps his surrounding culture didn't send him strong competing messages, or even ushered him along the asshole's path.

Perhaps, however, we needn't be able to identify a previous stage of life in which "full control" was exercised. It is enough, one might say, that we are each now fully in control of our-selves by virtue of powers that everyone beyond the age of rea-son enjoys: after a certain age, we may say, persons are suited to wholly determine their conduct, from a place outside culture and nature. That, we may say, is what freedom of will consists of. To the extent culture or nature has an influence, it merely shapes what we Freely Choose through and by our own Free-dom of Will.

The capitalized words are necessary here because it is noto-riously difficult to specify in further terms what the suggested powers would be. That isn't a fatal blow (in the end, not *every-thing* can be explained). The more important point is that, if we really want to underwrite our right to blame the asshole, this is not the surest guarantor. We can dogmatically assert the exis-tence of powers of Freedom of Will, pounding the table with our fist, but then dogmatism is all we are left with. When we then ask for a philosophical account of what is going on—even just a plausible sketch—it is pretty easy to be skeptical about whether anyone actually has powers to act into the order of nature and culture from someplace outside. In effect, we would have to be, like God, prime movers unmoved.[10] But is that really necessary? Should we really say that the asshole *must* be a prime mover simply in order to be appropriately blamed for an insulting remark? Maybe this breathtaking view of human nature will turn out to be true. But it is a tall order to insist that it *must* be true in order for us to be rightly pissed off at an asshole who parked his luxury car in two parking places.

That, at any rate, is reason to look into less dramatic proposals about the basic preconditions of blame. The asshole must indeed have freedom of will. But this is just to say that he must be the sort of person who is properly *credited* with his acts as his own. His behavior must be properly attributed to *him*, rather than to the world around him or to so many subpersonal forces—whether homunculi or states of his brain—at work in his head. Here it won't suffice that the person *behaves* in certain ways, whether in the spontaneous and "free" ways that all animals move or in involuntary bodily functions or knee-jerk reactions. The behavior of my arm going up only counts as my *action*—as *my* raising my arm, instead of my arm's being pushed from behind—when it reflects my intentions. My intention to raise my arm will usually be based in what I take to be some sort of reason, a reason I could often give you if you asked why I did what I did (e.g., I raise my arm in order to reach for a jelly jar or

10. This view is defended by Roderick M. Chisholm, "Human Freedom and the Self," in *Free Will,* 2nd ed., ed. Gary Watson (Oxford: Oxford University Press, 2003), 26.

in order to vote "aye" in a meeting). But, we suggest, to be the kind of person who is suited for such intentional conduct is all that is necessary for a person to be properly credited with and potentially blameworthy for his or her deeds. For the asshole to be the appropriate object of blame he must be the sort of person who *does what he does for what he thinks are good reasons*. As long as he is motivated to act by his own sense of what are or are not good enough reasons for action, as long as he would defend them as good enough for action if he were asked, his deeds are *his*. When he's done well, then he's rightly thanked or praised. When his assumed reasons are not in fact good enough, he's rightly to blame.

To elaborate, our basic theory in chapter 1 says, in effect, that the asshole has a certain view about what reasons he has or doesn't have. Fully cooperative people take themselves to have sufficient reason to abide by the expectations of conduct that normally apply among moral equals. The fact that such expectations require something is regarded not only as a good reason for action but as a reason that is good enough to outweigh or rule out other competing considerations, such as the inconvenience of acting in the expected way. The asshole shares this view of *other people's* reasons for action but makes an exception of himself by insisting that the normally applicable expectations do not, in his case, apply. To summarize, here, then, is the asshole's view of things:

> *Thinking Like an Asshole*: The man takes it as given (perhaps subconsciously or inchoately) that he is justified in allowing himself special advantages in social relations, in light of his special entitlement to them. That is, his sense of special entitlement tells him that he has *no reason or*

insufficient reason to abide by the expectations of conduct
that normally apply among moral equals.

So while the fully cooperative person takes there to be good
and normally sufficient reasons to queue up in good order when
a line has formed, the asshole sees no reason he should wait,
or at least no reason sufficiently good to justify the inconvenience. His line-cutting action is thus *his* action, simply because
it reflects his normative views: he'd defend them if we asked
him why he thought it should be acceptable. To the extent he
is also wrong about what reasons he has or doesn't have, to the
extent he has a mistaken normative perspective, he is the appropriate object of blame. He is the appropriate object of blame
just because he thinks like an asshole, just because his actions
flow from that (mistaken) set of moral views. He is to blame
because, in that attitudinal sense, he fails to recognize others as
the equals they are, by failing to recognize what treating them
as equals calls for.

PSYCHOPATHS AND MORAL BLINDNESS

In our proposal, the asshole is blameworthy because of a failure
of seeing. But here one might object that the bare fact of *having
certain mistaken moral views* cannot be the whole story. It might
seem to matter *why* the asshole fails to see what he fails to see.
Suppose, for instance, that he is morally blind, really and truly
incapable of taking in the appropriate facts about what he has
most reason to do or not do. Would he not then be off the moral
hook? If so, then when he is *on* the hook, it follows that he *has*
certain capacities to figure out what moral reasons he in fact
has. The asshole would then be blameworthy only because he *in*

fact has that moral capacity, where this is something more than *simply* having asshole moral views. No capacity, no responsibility. "Ought," as they say, implies "can."

The philosopher Gary Watson presents an argument like this one as regards the psychopath.[11] As Watson reads the psychological evidence, psychopaths are marked by two key features:

(1) they act with malice, deliberately and callously harming others, without coercion or psychosis; and

(2) they are incapable of recognizing the interests of others as claims on their conduct.

The fact that psychopaths act with malice, as according to (1), means they are unlike mere animals that must be controlled but cannot be blamed. It feels natural for us to *blame* the psychopath for a horrific murder and indeed to want to hold him accountable for his conduct, whether through punishment, strong criticism, or indignation. On the other hand, Watson argues, the fact that psychopaths are *incapable* of recognizing others as sources of valid claims on their conduct, as according to (2), means that ways of seeking to hold them accountable to moral expectations are misplaced. We therefore find them deeply disquieting. We recoil in indignation at the callous murders committed by Robert Alton Harris (he kidnapped, taunted, and shot two teenagers, then bragged about it while finishing

11. Gary Watson, "The Trouble with Psychopaths," in *Reasons and Recognition: Essays on the Philosophy of T. M. Scanlon,* ed. R. Jay Wallace, Rahul Kumar, and Samuel Freeman (New York: Oxford University Press, 2011). See also Watson's "Responsibility and the Limits of Evil: Variations on a Strawsonian Theme," in *Perspective on Moral Responsibility,* ed. John Martin Fischer and Mark Ravizza (Ithaca, NY: Cornell University Press, 1993), 119.

the lunches they had been eating). But we can also find ourselves in a more detached, objective mode when we think through his truly terrible upbringing. We naturally waffle on whether he is in fact morally responsible, depending on whether we think of the child he was or the man he became.[12] Ultimately, though, the psychopath isn't responsible, because he finally isn't capable of seeing that he owes people something better.

For our purposes, it is crucial to understand why Watson thinks the psychopath's inability to see the force of moral claims means that resentment or indignation is misplaced: his moral incapacity means there is no possibility of getting through, no possibility of getting him to even *understand,* let alone accept, that he has reason to respect the moral claims of others. But, according to Watson, the act of seeking to *hold someone account-able,* as opposed to simply trying to deter future bad behavior or otherwise keep him under control, is precisely that of trying to elicit an *internal* understanding and acceptance that the claims of others bear on his conduct. Reactive feelings such as resentment and indignation, for Watson, have just this implicit goal: to get their target to listen and understand. That means that resenting a psychopath is ultimately misplaced. It is in a basic way like Mr. Magoo's "ordering" a fence post to get off his property. A message is sent but cannot be received.[13]

In a moment we will apply this argument to the asshole, albeit in a localized way. We should first consider why the argument doesn't apply as it stands. As we noted in chapter 2, the main way the asshole differs from the psychopath is that the asshole is capable of using moral concepts and is motivated to

---

12. Watson, "Responsibility and the Limits of Evil."
13. Watson, "The Trouble with Psychopaths."

action by his use of them.[14] He might reason impeccably when his interests aren't at stake, and in a normatively engaged way. He can advise a friend about whether a certain debt should be repaid or promise kept, and he takes offense at a transgression in a way that shows his ability to appreciate the transgressed expectations as providing powerful reasons for action. His moral reasoning and its motivational pull are distorted only when *he* figures in the practical equation, when it then matters that he has entitlements that others (such as the advised friend) do not enjoy. Even then, he might reason just fine about his own actions on a good day or be generally reliable, say, in his family life. (Most assholes are not complete assholes. While assholes are generally "systematic" across many social contexts, only those who are assholes in almost every area of life are *complete assholes*.) What makes an asshole an asshole is the *way* he uses his real moral capacity. He puts that capacity in the dedicated service of confidence in his entitlement to special advantages by reasoning morally but without morality's impartiality.

We are admitting, then, that the asshole has certain *general* moral capacities of judgment and motivation. Is this to revise our initial proposal that the asshole is blameworthy simply because he has certain moral views? Not exactly. That proposal took for granted that the views are indeed *his* views, in a certain robust sense: they must be "attributable" to him, in current philosophical parlance. We are saying that *general* moral capacities come along with the package, but that isn't yet to say—and this

14. Some philosophers find it intelligible that a person could have moral concepts but stand unmoved by his own moral judgments, perhaps because he does not see them as supplying him with any reason for action. I'm inclined to classify this character as a psychopath rather than as an asshole. The asshole not only uses moral concepts but is motivated by his use of them, albeit in a deeply egocentric way.

is crucial for present purposes—that the asshole has capacities to see *specific* things in a certain situation (e.g., not to speak too loudly in public) as required of him.

To probe further: if a sense of entitlement to cut in line were implanted in your mind by a nefarious neuroscientist, it would not necessarily reflect *your* moral views, even if it effectively prompted you to cut into the line at the post office. The action is still not yours in the sense needed to blame *you* for doing this particular deed. (We might blame the neuroscientist instead; *he* made you do it.) So if the asshole's views are to be his own, they have to be part of his mind in the right way; they have to be owned or his own. And since they are *moral* views (about his special entitlements), they have to come along with any general capacities of moral reasoning needed for us to intelligibly ascribe to the asshole any moral attitudes at all. Philosophers call this the "holism" of the mental. In general, attitudes are always *someone's* attitudes. (Thus Descartes could infer his existence from his thoughts, with *cogito, ergo sum,* "I think, therefore I am.") But attitudes such as thoughts, beliefs, and feelings do not come one attitude at a time. We intelligibly ascribe any particular attitude to a person (e.g., a moral belief) only against the background of a web of other attitudes, the web needed for the ascription to make sense as part of a person's point of view (other moral attitudes and capacities). It sometimes *seems* that we have a wholly alien thought or feeling, wholly disconnected from anything else we think or feel (e.g., a passing thought of hitting someone one deeply respects over the head), but Freud nicely explained how we can usually tell a story that makes sense of a seemingly alien attitude, whether in terms of a deeper past or things below the surface of conscious awareness. (And, yes, as Freud suggested, it might somehow be about sex. After all, what isn't?)

Now, even if assholes have certain general moral capacities, we can still apply Watson's argument about psychopaths in a restricted way. If the asshole is to be properly held responsible for cutting in line, we may say, it isn't sufficient that he has *general* capacities to reason morally. He needs the *specific* capacity to see the particular moral reasons he has not to do the particular thing we blame him for doing; he must be able to see his particular reasons not to cut into this particular line, in this train station, on this afternoon. But now suppose that some asshole *can't* see that he is not special when it comes to line cutting, or line cutting in this particular place, or on this particular day. Perhaps that inability results from something in his distant past; he was raised with terrible beatings under oppressive rules and so now bucks against social rules, or—more likely these days—he was constantly told that he could do no wrong, that he and everything he did were completely wonderful.[15] Now further suppose we are trying to hold this asshole accountable, where this means trying to get him to understand and perhaps accept that he has sufficient reason to wait in line like everyone else. Well, in that case, ex hypothesi, he won't get it. Since he won't be able to understand, it will be misguided to demand that he see things otherwise, just as it will be pointless to morally argue with a psychopath and confused for Mr. Magoo to give orders to a fence post.

What should we say here? Troubling implications loom. Could an asshole simply be making a lot of these innocent mistakes and so never or rarely be an inappropriate object of blame?

15. For this general kind of argument, about moral incapacity due to upbringing, see Susan Wolf, "Sanity and the Metaphysics of Responsibility," in Watson, *Free Will,* 372–87.

Could his entrenched sense of entitlement *itself* make him incapable of seeing that he owes it to others to wait in line? Could he be blameless for being an asshole *precisely because he is an asshole*?

If that did follow, it would be so odd that we should assume something has gone awry. A good strategy for getting out of a muddle is to carefully review one's assumptions. To do that, we might ask what is wrong with simply taking a hard line: it makes no difference, we may say, whether or not the asshole has a specific capacity to see what others are particularly owed. We have sufficient grounds for blaming the asshole for cutting in line in the mere fact that he does so while being motivated by certain moral views; he thinks like an asshole, with whatever *general* moral capacities come along with that sort of moral point of view. As for why he is special when he cuts in line, he mainly makes something up. Simply having his faulty moral perspective is *itself enough* to render him a proper object of blame, even if he can't see the moral line-cutting situation in a different way.

To see how this might be right, consider more carefully what *blaming* the asshole might include. It might of course involve openly addressing him with a specific communicative message, such as "Hey, asshole, there's a line here. Get to the back of it, asshole." But there are other ways of blaming. You could avert your eyes when he approaches with a smile. You could refuse to shake his hand. You might withdraw a posture of goodwill that would have otherwise made you hope that things go well for him. You might even resent him, or well up with indignation, but without trying to send him a message of disapproval. You might be resentful or indignant without trying to get him to understand or accept your rightful claims or equal moral status. All these reactions seem to count as ways of blaming him. But none of them depends upon the assumption that he isn't, in a particular case, simply morally blind. You could avoid him, withdraw goodwill, or resent him all the same.[16]

If that seems promising, we might then question why *accountability* should take center stage. Suppose Watson is quite correct that holding someone to account involves an implicit demand that the addressed person recognize one's status and rightful claims. We are suggesting that one can still rightly blame the asshole, in any number of ways, without trying to hold him accountable. We can even explain why holding the asshole to account should seem to matter: it is a way of seeking recognition, a way of trying to get him to see that we or others are owed certain things. But, as we will see in chapter 5, the quest for recognition needn't take only that form. Even if the asshole will not or even cannot listen, a minor act of protest can be a way of recognizing oneself by affirming one's claim to better treatment in a way that any reasonable onlooker would agree with. One might simply swear "asshole!" under one's breath or in mere thought, for much the same reason one swears out loud while alone in a car: the swearing is itself a way of taking a stand. We can blame and seek recognition, then, whether or not we try to hold him accountable.[17]

16. This is T. M. Scanlon's view in "Blame," in *Moral Dimensions: Permissibility, Meaning, Blame* (Cambridge: Belknap Press of Harvard University Press, 2008). Our suggestion is that this view fits the asshole, which might be true even if Watson is right that it doesn't fit the psychopath. For a related view of "attributability," see Angela M. Smith, "Responsibility for Attitudes: Activity and Passivity in Mental Life," *Ethics* 115 (2005): 236–71.

17. Which is not to say Watson is right that an asshole could not be properly held accountable if he suffered from local moral blindness. (I myself am not sure.) We sidestep that further issue here.

BLAMING INCORRIGIBLES

Our basic proposal, then, is that the asshole is properly blamed simply because he thinks like an asshole—that is, because he has certain mistaken moral views about what he is entitled to. He may even be incapable of seeing, in a particular situation, that he has good and sufficient reason to abide by the particular expectations that normally govern moral equals. Even with such moral blind spots, he is rightly blamed for those very errors in judgment.

We should now consider a different way of resisting this conclusion. One may say that, even if the asshole is incapable of seeing in some particular case, his failure may and often will *trace back* to his earlier decisions about how seriously to take the claims of others. The asshole is responsible for his particular failure of seeing, in this view, because it reflects that *earlier* morally culpable decision, much in the way one may be blameworthy for drunk driving and the consequent death of a child because one decided to get behind the wheel instead of calling a cab.

There is something to this, which we will explore in a moment. Yet to say that this is the *only* way an asshole can be responsible for his moral blind spots would be to unduly limit when we can blame him. The asshole must then have at some point made a previous decision that explains how he could now be morally oblivious much of the time. But the appropriateness of resenting the guy who has just swerved through three lanes of traffic does not seem to depend on the assumption that he decided to be a guy of that kind in a clear-eyed moment of choice an hour or year or decade before.[18] He needn't even have negligently overlooked how his life would affect others in any grand decision about what kind of person to be. As we suggested above, many assholes are overgrown teenagers who never faced up to the morality of disregarding others in any general and conscious way. (They certainly won't have chosen a life under the description "life of disregarding others." They might have said to themselves, "Fuck them!," which comes to much the same thing.) Still, these assholes are rightly blamed, even if they can't now see their reasons not to treat others as equals, and even if they never made a decision to become morally oblivious in this way.

Is this unfair? Is it unfair to blame the asshole for failing to see things he perhaps cannot see, as a result of being a kind of person he may have never decided to become? No, this isn't unfair at all: we treat non-assholes on the same terms. Everyone has the occasional moral lapse. There is something we just didn't see (I should have said "thank you." I should have been more careful with a friend's confidences). Perhaps one *couldn't* have seen without hindsight. Still, one is rightly blamed. The friend with compromised confidences will be miffed, and one will naturally apologize for the mistake. That is true even when one has generally made a huge effort at conscientiousness, being on the lookout for important things one knows one doesn't yet know. Such larger efforts will *mitigate* blame in a given lapse, perhaps to an extent that no one will make a big deal of it. Perhaps the lapse doesn't seem especially reflective of the person

18. For a version of this argument in light of "Jeff the jerk," see Manuel R. Vargas, "The Trouble with Tracing," *Midwest Studies in Philosophy* 29 (2005): 269–91.

more generally, and friends will blow it off by saying that "everyone makes mistakes." Still, we are indeed blameworthy for the lapse, only to a lesser extent. That is why we apologize.

Compare the jerk or the schmuck. We blame him for his particular failures of seeing, and we take them to be *exacerbated* by his more general failure to make an effort at improving his moral sight. In that sense, what might otherwise be a normal lapse *does* reflect the person's jerky or schmucky nature. He may even be incorrigible in this. He may not defend this lackadaisical attitude and may even apologize for it—before being just as carefree over the next day or week. But it is not that we blame him for his particular failures of seeing *only* because we blame him for his more general way of being. We simply blame him for both.

Like the jerk or schmuck, the asshole fails to recognize the particular moral claims of others *and* he makes no general effort at coming to better see what people are owed. The asshole is to blame for his particular failures of seeing no less than we are to blame for our particular moral lapses. As with the jerk and the schmuck, the asshole's particular errors are exacerbated and possibly explained by his general failure to make any effort at improving his moral sight. In the case of the asshole, however, the general failure reflects his entrenched *resistance* to moral learning. It reflects his (perhaps inchoate) sense that *he doesn't have to make those sorts of efforts*. Given his special standing, it is only natural that the special advantages of social life should flow his way. We thus blame the asshole for his situational errors *and* for the basic error that defines his very way of being.

Of course, the occasional asshole does change his way of being. Dickens's Ebenezer Scrooge eventually undergoes a dramatic moral transformation.[19] It is an interesting question whether assholes ever wholly transform, or whether being an asshole is more like a being an alcoholic: one is always gratefully in recovery and never finally cured. Nor would an eleventh-hour "transformation," as death approaches, clearly qualify; it may be better to say that the dying man is understandably just not being himself. I would guess the transformation can be and sometimes is total. This is not, however, why assholes are properly blamed: assholes aren't to blame because they can potentially recover. They are to blame simply because they think like an asshole, whether or not they will, or even can, ever change.

19. Three different Jack Nicholson characters, in *As Good as It Gets, About Schmidt,* and *Something's Gotta Give,* eventually come into self-knowledge that mitigates their assholish condition.

[5] ASSHOLE MANAGEMENT

We have said that an asshole can be beyond moral correction and yet still be the appropriate object of blame. That is not yet to say how he is best handled. How, aside from merely placing blame, should we respond to the annoying man who has just interrupted, or woven across three traffic lanes, or created a giant political mess?

Much of the rest of this book is about asshole management, or, more accurately, why asshole management is unavoidably difficult. In chapter 6, we look at the difficulty of limiting the profusion of assholes throughout society. In this chapter, our topic is personal asshole management and the special way assholes destabilize small groups.

SELF-UNDERSTANDING AS SELF-HELP

When it comes to personal asshole management, there is unfortunately very little useful to say by way of self-help—certainly nothing like an eleven-step guide to an asshole-free life. The asshole is deeply bothersome because we find it difficult to even *understand* what a good, constructive response would be, let alone to actually produce it on the spot. Despite many hard lessons about what did not work, and perhaps even the odd success, it takes only a fresh kind of asshole—or just the same old sort of asshole, encountered at a bad time—to catch one unawares, throw one off balance, and spoil one's whole day.

One's day is spoiled because one feels forced into either of two unpalatable responses: a demeaning acquiescence or a personally disappointing and ineffectual fit of rage. That is, on the one hand, we have the option of *resignation*: we give in to what is plainly mistreatment, allow ourselves to be taken advantage of, and find reasons to somehow make this feel okay. On the other hand, we have the option of *resistance*: we stand up for ourselves and fight to be morally recognized. But fighting back can seem an exercise in futility. No amount of angry protest will get a true asshole to listen. As we explained in chapter 1, he is *entrenched* in his outlook; he is exceedingly good at walling out complaints, and, in this, he will most likely never change. Although neither resignation nor all-out resistance seems finally acceptable, we often have only the faintest sense of an ever-elusive better way.

Our best hope for finding that better way is to better understand ourselves. Why do we find both resignation and all-out resistance ultimately acceptable? The answer lies in the importance we attach to the kind of treatment the asshole deprives us of—that is, the importance of being morally recognized as an equal in the eyes of others. As we will now see, this explains why neither resignation nor all-out resistance is the best course, and in a way that points us toward more productive ways of seeking to be recognized.

RESIGNATION AND THE LOSS
OF SELF-RESPECT

To begin, we might ask, What was so bad about resignation? To someone frustrated, one might offer the following counsel:

"Take it easy. The guy is just an asshole. Why be so worried about what an *asshole* thinks?" One might elaborate with counsels of productivity: "And in any case, you've got better things to do with your time. Just give the asshole what he wants, what he thinks he deserves, and be done with it. It helps in this to temporarily buy his view of the world. Throw in an ego stroke, just for good measure. An asshole who feels that you completely understand him is much more likely to leave you alone."

Unless of course he doesn't leave you alone, which he often won't. (Perhaps he now feels he can take more and more of what he was anyway after.) There is good advice in these counsels of productivity, yet the stated version cannot be entirely right. For one thing, in the face of a persistent, wearing asshole, the advice is exceedingly difficult to follow. Our feelings of revulsion, of anger, and of a thirst for retribution are not consciously chosen or readily set to one side. They come unbidden. Reactive feelings do not simply arise in the moment of confrontation. They can intrude upon a pleasant sunny day, in a flashing image of the man in question suddenly breaking out in a rash, of his losing bladder control in a public place, of his convulsing from having eaten poisoned food, of his being mowed down by a truck, of his being crushed by a meteor, or of fluids spraying spontaneously out of all his orifices (onto his friends standing nearby).[1] Until of course one realizes, on second thought, that a person staring into the abyss may not be reflecting on his lack of concern for others, which may in turn prompt either a more elaborate scheme of revenge or, instead, a natural understanding of

---

1. Likewise, in many murder mysteries the victim is portrayed as an asshole. We thus feel he "had it coming," as, e.g., with Dickens's character Tulkinghorn in *Bleak House*.

how a Day of Judgment in the afterlife should have such endur-
ing human appeal and, relatedly, of how there could be a moral
basis to most religious metaphysics. We don't have to believe
that the asshole will actually get his in the end to find ourselves,
passively and disappointingly, wrapped up a fantasized vengeful
plot. Perhaps that isn't so bad, because we of course would never
go through with the fantasy. Or would we?

Being overtaken by obsessive rumination can seem like a personal flaw or, in the extreme, a psychological disorder. Yet it isn't.
The retributive feelings are a natural if extreme way of affirming one's right to better treatment, a way of reassuring oneself
of one's equal moral status. Ultimately, reactive feelings reflect
good and proper self-respect. We do well to tutor how they are
expressed, perhaps by reminding ourselves that there is nothing
good, as such, in human suffering, even an asshole's human suffering. But there is nothing regrettable or reproachable in a natural affirmation of basic self-worth. If we *could* somehow ease
ourselves out of that affirmative disposition—whether through
years of patient mediation, a brutal process of cognitive psycho-
therapy, or by rewiring the limbic brain and basal ganglia—we'd
be well advised not to go through with it. We'd be carving away
at something not all too human, but only human, and therefore
something properly respected or even cherished.

In much the same way, and for the same reasons, people
strongly, often violently resist being played for a sucker: better
to fight than be someone's lackey. The trouble, especially for
men, is that resistance is easily overdone, bringing its own set
of problems. Consider a man who has laser clarity that "no one
fucks with me," given an expansive definition of the "fucking
with" relation, which includes such things as looking at him
wrong, turning one's head in the general direction of his woman,

or being too tall (and so in need of being taken down). This view finds sophisticated expression in the great political theorist Thomas Hobbes's expansive right of self-defense, which includes a right of anticipatory strikes against anyone one deems a potential enemy.[2] Much the same view finds more recent expression in the Bush doctrine of preventive war and its use in justifying the invasion of Iraq, on the basis of what turned out to be whispered rumors of WMDs. Morally, these versions of the right of self-defense are a stretch.[3] Yet we can certainly appreciate their source: no one wants to be a sucker, and, from a moral point of view, we just don't have to stand by and allow ourselves to be taken advantage of by an asshole.

When we are at risk of being exploited, we can at least take ourselves out of the asshole's way. Which suggests a strategy of vigilant avoidance: if one plans with sufficient foresight, one can systematically avoid putting oneself in a position to encounter an asshole. One can be exceedingly careful about whom one befriends, dates, and marries; one can work for oneself and forgo business deals with anyone who might be suspect; and so on. Yet this surely goes too far. Should one avoid or leave

2. Thomas Hobbes, *Leviathan*, ed. Richard Tuck (Cambridge: Cambridge University Press, 1996), chap. 13.

3. The Bush doctrine reads that "America will act against . . . emerging threats before they are fully formed" (p. 4 of Bush's National Security Strategy of the United States of America). This does address real questions about how the requirement in international law of a "credible and imminent" threat of attack (is a terrorism plot ten years in the making "imminent"?). But it also rejects, or at least fails to admit, even minimal moral expectations, for instance, that there should at least be solid evidence of a threat. According to the doctrine, an "emerging threat" that isn't "fully formed" needn't even be especially "credible" before preventive strikes are launched. In effect, then, there is no real limit on the use of violence at all.

Italy, along with all its bounteous joys, simply because one can be pretty confident that an asshole will cut you off in traffic or drive behind an ambulance to save time in traffic? Should one pass on one's favored career in banking or academia because one will be stuck dealing with an asshole from time to time? Surely not. We all manage our associations to some extent already. The single-minded pursuit of asshole avoidance would come at a too high a cost.

In that case, one will invariably have to cooperate within social interactions that the asshole exploits. But how can one cooperate without being a sucker? We surely don't have to stand up to every asshole. This is, again, a good counsel of productivity: it isn't worth it to fight every good fight; as the point is often put, "you have to pick your battles." But to *never* stand up for oneself, to always acquiesce, also seems mistaken or, for most, even impossible. We can and should fight for our rights at *some* point. The question, then, is in what way. The question is how to fight for recognition without lashing out.

RESISTANCE WITHOUT WAR

Let us turn then to our second and opposing reaction: all-out resistance. Here we immediately face a difficulty. How could fighting for moral recognition possibly be a worthy cause if the asshole *will not listen,* by his very nature, try as we might to get through? How could an *exercise in futility* be worthwhile?

It might be said that we often won't be certain that the man in front of us is a proper asshole who will not or cannot change. He *could* be a borderline case and might be moved by one's protest. Calling him an asshole could give him pause. It could be that he has never thought of himself in that light and, now being forced to look at himself in a different way, feels ashamed. If there's a chance he'll listen, why not try?

While this is fine as far as it goes, it mainly postpones our problem. When a first effort is made and rebuffed, should you now continue to seek recognition, persisting in the good fight? Or should you simply give up? Especially when we are stuck in repeated encounters with an asshole who wears on our nerves, we presumably should stand up for our rights instead of simply letting the asshole have his way with us. But how could that be worthwhile if any quest for recognition is bound to fail? Why aren't we left with an unacceptable choice between resigning ourselves to being a sucker and an arduous and probably futile struggle to uphold our rights?

The answer to this question is that we are not forced to choose between acquiescence and all-out resistance. One can stand up for one's rights in many constructive and fruitful ways short of trying to do the impossible—get the asshole to listen and change.

To see this, consider why we swear out loud at the asshole in traffic. We often *know* that he cannot hear us in his car. Indeed, we are especially prone to do this while driving alone (because passengers may be disturbed or offended), knowing full well that *no one* else can hear. Is there a point to this? Is it simply that there is pleasure in venting, the gratification of a cathartic, ejaculatory burst? No, or at least not entirely. We do this, rather, in order to *recognize ourselves,* as a proxy for the recognition of others. We are reassuring ourselves that we do deserve better treatment and that this is something that any reasonable onlooker, were one present, would agree with.

The phenomenon reflects our more general need to keep ourselves intelligible to others. Consider, by comparison, "response cries" such as *aha, bleh, eeuw, goody, hmph, oh, oops, phew, whee, yikes,* or *yuck*. Why do we spontaneously blurt out these words, often in a moment of awkwardness? As psychologist and linguist Steven Pinker explains, we do so with others in mind:

> A person who knocks over a glass might be a klutz, but if he says *whoops,* then at least we know that he didn't intend the outcome and regrets that it happened. A person who says *yuck* after dripping pizza sauce on his shirt or stepping in dog feces is someone we understand better than someone who seems not to care.

Following sociologist Erving Goffman, Pinker suggests that we do this in order to "signal our competence and shared understanding of the situation to a generic audience," where the audience may be imagined rather than real:[4]

> One goal . . . is to reassure onlookers that we are sane, competent, reasonable human beings, with transparent goals and intelligible responses to the current situation. Ordinarily this requires that we not talk to ourselves in public, but we make an exception when a sudden turn of events puts our rationality or effectiveness to the test. My favorite example is when we do an about-face in a hallway and mutter a soliloquy explaining to no one in particular that we forgot something in our office, as if to reas-

4. Steven Pinker, *The Stuff of Thought: Language as a Window into Human Nature* (New York: Viking Press, 2007), 366–67 (including the list of response cries given earlier). Pinker cites Erving Goffman, *The Presentation of Self in Everyday Life* (New York: Doubleday, 1959).

sure any onlookers that we are not a lunatic who lurches around at random.

The same goes for swearing out loud in the car. Pinker says cathartic swearing is a response to a "sudden challenge to our goals or well-being." But that isn't quite right; swearing with the term "asshole" is a response specifically to a *person*. Pinker himself notes in passing that "people shout *Asshole!* when they suffer a sudden affront from a human perpetrator, but not when they pick up a hot casserole or have a mousetrap snap on their finger."[5] Our theory explains why we swear *only* at persons: the concept of an asshole is essentially keyed to states of mind that only persons can have, in particular, the attitudes and dispositions involved in conducting oneself in a way that reflects one's appreciation of others as fellow persons and moral equals. That does not itself explain why we call an asshole an asshole when we know that he won't care. But we now have our explanation. When the asshole has failed to give us our due in traffic, we swear out loud, not to get *him* to listen but to reassure ourselves that others, real or imagined, would hear our case and agree. We in effect tell ourselves that if he won't uphold our status as a moral equal, everyone else will.

So swearing is, in a small way, a means of upholding one's rights, seen as a kind of public status or standing. In that case, one can equally take a performative stand without harsh words. When an asshole is loudly talking on his cell phone for a long time with others around, one might say out loud: "Sir, given your

5. Pinker, *The Stuff of Thought*, 366. Oddly, although one wouldn't cry "asshole" in kicking a step, one might say "son of a bitch," even though that term seems to refer to a type of person.

cell phone behavior, I'm tempted not simply to ask you to keep it down but to inject a cutting remark or perhaps speak of you in less dignified words." When the asshole chuckles and brushes the comment off, and even when he lashes out, it won't undermine the point of having spoken up. (Some intelligent assholes will respect and appreciate a clever or stylish response and perhaps even feel greater respect for the person, if perhaps only for a short while.) Speaking up will be worthwhile in itself, if only to affirm the fact that speaking up is indeed now within one's rights and a reflection of one's standing, as a moral equal, to stand up and complain. Moreover, the others in line will appreciate having *their* rights publicly upheld for all to hear. Everyone (except the asshole) is then reassured that everyone sees that everyone deserves better and that everyone can reasonably complain. With that shared understanding reaffirmed, it can even then make sense to forgo efforts to change or stop the asshole. There may be better things to do with the time, such as have a fun conversation about what an asshole that guy was, about whether there are more assholes than there used to be, and so on.

In short, the good fight for recognition is as much a fight for a *public status* as for anything else. It is not simply a struggle to get this particular man, on this particular day, to recognize one as an equal. Even when that isn't in the cards, working to publicly uphold one's rights or the rights of others *is* often worth fighting for, in any number of large and small ways.

The point of speaking up is much like the point of nonviolent protest, for instance, as during apartheid in South Africa (where Gandhi first developed the practice of nonviolent civil disobedience). The goal of peacefully taking to the streets was not *simply* to persuade the entrenched white minority in power, who had already shown an extraordinary ability to wall out any reasons for racial desegregation. The goal was also to invite the larger South African public, including many potentially sympathetic whites, to appreciate the rightful claims of segregated minorities without using violence in a way that would trigger their defenses and close their ears.

To be sure, the protests against apartheid wanted major institutional change, and that required actually bringing around a certain number of elite asshole whites (or at least a sufficient number of *borderline* asshole whites, so that the proper and deeply resistant assholes were marginalized). Yet protest would not have been entirely pointless, even if major institutional change was assumed to be hopeless. Peaceful protest might make perfect sense as a last stand. So might self-inflicted violence. The South Korean rice farmer who stabbed himself to death at the 2003 Cancun World Trade Organization meeting, in order to protest rich-world farm subsidies that impoverish developing-world farmers, needn't have thought that his desperate act would usher in major institutional change. Public recognition of the plight of poor farmers might have been his whole point.

Such dramatic interventions are not the normal mode of asshole protestation. It will be unreasonable and unwise to take to the streets every time one is slighted. Nor will there always be an audience to protest for. Even swearing out loud, for oneself, may be less effective than stony silence, an averted gaze, or conspicuous failure to cooperatively engage when one otherwise would (for instance, by refusing to bend over to pick up the asshole's pen or paperwork dropped at one's feet after he has cut in the post office line). A small silent protest may speak loudly, even if not to the asshole who refuses to hear. It may succeed as a self-affirmation as much as swearing out loud. Indeed, while swearing out loud puts one's own dignity at risk, perhaps as much as doing nothing at all, a dignified protest in the small is nearly always possible and often worthwhile.

HITTING THE SWEET SPOT

All this is to say *that* there is space between acquiescence and all-out resistance, not *how* one is to reliably hit that sweet spot. There is no general recipe or procedure for actually doing this, even once we know that moral recognition is what we are after. Still, for what it is worth, here are two suggestions.

The first is: don't try to change the asshole, and cooperate only on your own terms. The second is: take a stand at the right time. We take each suggestion in turn.

OWN YOUR ATTITUDES

According to a Stoic principle, one must always accept what is given. One can hope for good things and work toward them, but one should not strive for what is not within one's power. As the wise Epictetus explains, "If [a way things appear] concerns anything outside of your control, train yourself not to worry about it."[6]

Among things not within one's control Epictetus explicitly includes the recognition or lack of recognition by others. He writes:

6. Epictetus, *A Manual for Living*, trans. Sharon Lebell (New York: Harper-Collins, 1994), 12.

> It is only after you have . . . learned to distinguish between
> what you can and can't control that inner tranquility and
> outer effectiveness become possible. . . . Such things
> as . . . *how we are regarded by others* . . . are externals and
> therefore not our concern.[7]

Since one can't change an asshole, then, one shouldn't try.
One shouldn't seek recognition in his eyes.

Now, the Stoics arguably take this too far. They famously
counsel that one can retain happy equanimity even while being
stretched on the rack or in the face of the death of your own
child. One need only adjust one's interpretations of how things
appear. It should then be relatively easy to accept being taken
advantage of by an asshole. As Epictetus explains:

> People don't have the power to hurt you. Even if someone
> shouts abuse at you or strikes you, if you are insulted, it
> is always your choice to view what is happening as insult-
> ing or not. If someone irritates you, it is only your own
> response that is irritating you. Therefore, when anyone
> seems to be provoking you, remember that it is only your
> judgment of the incident that provokes you.[8]

Indeed, as Epictetus elaborates, it is the provocateur who is
mainly injured:

> If someone treats you disrespectfully or speaks unkindly
> about you, remember that he or she does so from [his or

7. Epictetus, *A Manual for Living*, 9–10, my italics.
8. Epictetus, *A Manual for Living*, 34–35.

her] impression that it is right to do so. It is unrealistic to expect that this person sees you as you see yourself. If another person reaches conclusions based on false impressions, he or she is the one hurt rather than you, because it is that person who is misguided.[9]

So we are to own our perceptions *as our own*. If nothing else, this is a good way of mellowing oneself out. Still, having mellowed, one might well finally conclude, on due reflection, that this guy is a serious asshole and that some response—perhaps a quick riposte—is indeed called for. It is only if there really is *nothing* one can do by way of reply that full disengagement becomes the wise course (as in "Here he goes again; let us observe whether his technique is changing, perhaps even improving!"). When constructive replies are in the cards, we will rightly take our chances on action. Epictetus might well agree, as long as action flows from full acceptance that the world may not cooperate. We should act decisively but stand ready to let go. Trying is fine, as long as it is not fruitless striving for what is not in our power.

What, then, should one try for? For the Stoics, the flip side of our lack of full control over the world is that we have correspondingly heightened personal responsibility for our *attitudes and interpretations,* which *are* within our power. A responsible reply to the asshole will seek after what is achievable and worthy. The practical challenge is to seek that and nothing more. The Stoics tell us how: we appropriately judge the appearances, through clear thinking. As Epictetus explains, "It is through

9. Epictetus, *A Manual for Living,* 78.

clear thinking that we are able to properly direct our will, stick with our true purpose, and discover the connections we have to others and the duties that follow from those relationships."[10] As we might put it, we are to seek *self-clarification*. We might start by mindfully considering how we are now feeling; what we are tempted to strive for; what seems difficult to let go of; and what the alternative thoughts, feelings, and plans would be. We then consider which reactions are ultimately just and worthwhile, settle upon that course, and stay with it. If a goal such as *getting the asshole to listen* or *teaching him the error of his ways* is tempting but unachievable or unworthy, we first identify that we are indeed, right now, drawn to acting for the sake of that particular end. Without self-judgment, we then let go of that particular goal and adopt a more worthy and more achievable aim, such as upholding our rights or the rights of others in a public way, without expecting the asshole to listen or change.

The possibility of self-clarification helps explain why we do not have to completely avoid the asshole, which we earlier said was often too costly. It can easily seem that, in cooperating with the asshole at all, one becomes complicit in one's own exploitation—a sucker—by sustaining the cooperative interactions the asshole takes advantage of. But this is not inevitable: one can cooperate on a footing of self-respect as long as one cooperates *on one's own terms*. One might allow oneself to have a conversation with the asshole, for instance, but without giving him the openness or the time that one would give to a friend or a nice stranger in a coffee shop. Such terms are *one's own* when they reflect one's own clearheaded judgment about the sorts

10. Epictetus, *A Manual for Living,* 80.

of engagements that are, for one's own reasons, worthwhile. If you have a light chat with the asshole because you think this helps to uphold a tone of civility at work, then, as long as you believe that *upholding civility is worthwhile,* you are not necessarily being co-opted into the asshole's normal ways—even as you may well be supporting one general form of cooperation that the asshole cheats.

We have said that one shouldn't try to get the asshole to listen. But now it might seem that this *could* be worth trying for. If one can cooperate with the asshole, why not at least *try* to get the asshole to eventually change? We usually won't know that *this* asshole won't give us the recognition we are owed. He is resistant—he is an asshole—but he might well budge, and there is always room for hope, perhaps against hope, that his walls will come down. Perhaps a failed stratagem will work the next time. Perhaps some new tack will get through. Perhaps persistent, patient resistance will eventually pay off. Shouldn't we at least then try? Even if it failed, wouldn't such an effort be worthwhile?

We suggest not, for reasons our initial counsel of productivity provided: for many of us as regards most assholes, the appropriate maxim is: "Don't waste your time." To adopt asshole reform as one's personal cause may well be fruitless. It will invariably mean forgoing more valuable things one could be doing instead, things such as listening to music, having coffee with a friend, or helping the poor. Add to that the persistent frustrations and struggle to stave off despair, and asshole reform will not make a lot of sense. To be sure, for some of us and some assholes, the cause might be sensible or indeed the only choice. Perhaps the asshole is one's husband or the father of one's child. Here Stoic wisdom suggests biding one's time and devising a cunning plan, a plan that finds a way of getting through while not simply enabling the asshole—all while steadily reminding oneself that success is ultimately not within one's power. For those in this difficult position, something more useful than a philosophical book about assholes will probably be required. It may help to love and forgive the asshole, to the extent that this is possible, perhaps in hope of his moral reform, assuming one can do that without losing one's self-respect.[11] Even so, it will be wise not to insist upon or labor for his reform.[12]

PROTEST, BUT SELECTIVELY

We thus have our first piece of advice: don't try to change the asshole, but feel free to cooperate on one's own terms. Our second piece of advice is: take a stand at the right time. We should speak up in protest, on behalf of oneself or others, but only (or at least mostly) at the right time. When is the right time? Our answer is "often enough"—that is, often enough to preserve one's self-respect and to uphold the rights of others when duty calls.

That answer isn't especially helpful. How often is often enough? When does duty call? But it is not clear that there can

11. For an account of how forgiveness is possible without loss of self-respect, see Pamela Hieronymi, "Articulating an Uncompromising Forgiveness," *Philosophy and Phenomenological Research* 62 (May 2001): 529–55.

12. The large percentage of the human population who claim to be Christians might seem to be in an especially difficult position. Christian love *requires* making asshole reform an organizing life cause. Indeed, one is to hope for *every* asshole's ultimate reform. In that case, Stoic wisdom counsels in favor of not trying to do what only an all-powerful God can get done. One can lend God a hand but rightly resist adopting *changing the asshole* as one's own final plan. Lending a hand might involve extraordinary vigilance and much prayer or simply leaving the asshole alone, perhaps in hope that God has some kind of plan.

be a more general rule, given that people have such different circumstances. Certain issues may require special vigilance by all; if the asshole is sexist, as many are, both women and men will need to reliably uphold the boundaries of respectful treatment, for example. But most cases are more complicated. Whether one should take a stand now might depend on what else one has going on that week. Someone dealing with a family crisis won't have time to stage a protest. Someone in a slow spell at work might. Moreover, people often have very different temperaments. Those stable in their sense of self-worth will find it easy to blow off the asshole's slights and only occasionally sound a protest. More sensitive types will need to persistently speak up.

THE MANAGEMENT ARTS

If we can do little more than offer general rules of thumb, which we have to use our best judgment to apply to the situation presented to us, we might at least explain why this should be so. This is to be expected: asshole management is less science and more art. It is less like following a procedure than having the knack for an art or a craft in Aristotle's sense: it can be learned only by doing, not by following rules that one could fully grasp ahead of time. Ideal asshole management is akin to the martial art of aikido, which allows one to absorb the force of one's attacker, by turning his own momentum against him, in order to protect oneself (and the attacker) from injury. Like asshole management, aikido cannot be fully grasped by any set of formulae; it must be learned by practice, usually over many years.

This also explains why hitting the sweet spot with the asshole is so difficult. We are surprised to see the aikido black belt swiftly disable a knifeman. The act shows a real possibility of reaction that otherwise wouldn't have seemed to be there.

One can learn to see and seize the possibility ahead of time but only with much practice over time. When we repeatedly fail to get our own response to the asshole correct, then we rightly give ourselves a break. In aikido, to demand that a yellow belt perform like a black or brown belt is unkind and unrealistic: it fails to appreciate how difficult learning the practice is. So we shouldn't expect perfect asshole management, even when we have given it more than a college try. Nor should we necessarily preoccupy ourselves with the mastery of this particular art. Here, again, the good counsels of productivity apply. Should you devote your life to asshole aikido? While that would not be entirely unworthy, there are probably better things to do with the limited time one has in life, things such as learning to paint large canvases in the abstract; refining one's taste in jazz; or, indeed, learning the martial art of aikido for the sake of the *practice* itself (rather than for the few occasions one will ever use it in a fight). Life affords only so much time, and there are better things to do—sweeter spots to hit—than perfection in the asshole management arts.

POISONING THE WELL

We have been considering asshole management in one-on-one encounters. We now turn to asshole management in a small group, where the difficulties can become especially acute. When people gather in shared purpose—say, at a boardroom meeting, in a small business, in a community construction project, or on a camping trip—this often brings a certain amount of fellow feeling and good vibes. The asshole poisons this well of goodwill by turning well-meaning people against one another. This puts him in the advantageous position of being able to prevent the group from cooperating so as to keep him under control.

To illustrate, consider a small business meeting and a certain major investor. Because he is a major investor, he cannot simply be expunged from the meeting. We are not now thinking of the merely "difficult person," or SOB, who is on balance a force for good, which we mentioned in chapter 2. The guy of our concern is mostly unproductive; he is not working with the group for the group's purposes, except when they merely happen to coincide with his. He is competing for attention; for his chance to comment on every comment; for control over the conversation's direction; and, ideally, for final say in the group's choice. Others will be vying for influence and power, to be sure, but mainly behind the scenes or at any rate with a good measure of civility. Our man is not always patently uncivil but not quite civil either; he can't quite hide the fact that, in his view, this is of course his meeting, that a decision he disagrees with would be completely outrageous and raise serious questions of retaliation. He needn't openly threaten retaliation, with memories fresh in the group from the last time things didn't go his way. The threat is now taken as a given by all and amply conveyed by his elevated tone or awkward glare.

In such a setting, the asshole's work is possible only because enough other people are upholding the cooperation he exploits. There would not be a meeting in the first place if the others didn't show up and more or less abide by meeting rules. The asshole is, in a sense, not just a person but a social *role* created within the loose structure of cooperation. The role could be assumed by a different person in the group when the chief asshole is on vacation. (The chief asshole will usually have established that he is the kingpin, having forced the secondary asshole to normally stand aside; otherwise, there won't be room in town for the both of them.)

The effective asshole usually appreciates the deeply social

nature of his work. He knows there are limits. People won't stand for deviancy that is too far beyond the pale. When people can readily agree that someone's conduct has become just too rank, just too outrageous, they will easily rally together and stand against it. This, according to Émile Durkheim, is the positive social function of deviancy: it helps rally the cooperative troops. But assholes aren't unwittingly productive in this way. They aren't rank deviants but rather deviants in the gray, hard-to-identify areas of cooperative life, where cooperative people easily disagree or fail to see the same things. Something feels wrong to all, but no one can quite make out exactly what it might be. Or if someone does see it, even plain as day, he or she won't know that others see it plainly as well. The fact that many others aren't getting it or aren't more bothered or, worse, are facilitating it can leave one not just upset at the asshole but sorely disappointed in one's fellows.

In a climate of heighted sensitivity and lack of conspicuous agreement, cooperative people can easily turn on one another. People have very strong feelings about the asshole but also about how others respond to him. Some involved seem to be enabling the asshole; they are being co-opted, taken for suckers. For many, this is disturbing to watch. How could they not stand up for themselves? If they must insist on being lackeys, why can't they do it on their own time, when they aren't enabling the asshole at the group's expense? A different type of person lashes out against the asshole, often for fear of being a sucker. This, too, is hard to accept. It can cause as much trouble as the asshole himself. With low-level combat being waged, the work of the group is not getting done.

Because these can be very strong feelings, a group of well-meaning people may easily divide over how the asshole should be handled, finding themselves in an uncivil peace. One coalition might favor taking a stand against the asshole at great cost, for the sake of the group's self-respect. A different faction might form around keeping the peace, even at a high price, so that the normal work of the group can carry on. Within each sub-group, the fellow members will find comfort in their agreement about how disappointing members of the opposing coalition have been lately. They may feel ever confident that theirs is the way forward and that it is the opposing coalition—and not really the asshole—that stands in progress's way. That obstinate group may seem almost as bad as the asshole himself, or maybe worse. Meanwhile, the shrewd asshole will carefully stoke these oppos-ing feelings and expand the scope of his powers.

THE FRAGILITY OF TOLERANCE

The natural solution is tolerance. The group must cultivate toler-ance of divergent reactions to a difficult problem; it must accept divergent asshole-management styles. With only a moment's reflection, cooperative people can all realize from their own experience how disturbing encounters with an asshole can be. They can all relate to feeling unable to muster a good response or suddenly finding oneself at one's worst. If the group can con-verge around this as a shared understanding, it will not be so readily destabilized. It will be readier to accept divergent reac-tions. It will be better able to find workable ways of together limiting the damage the asshole does.

There, however, is the rub: arriving at any such shared under-standing is *itself* a task for collective action, which is beyond the efforts of any one person taken by him or herself. No one can do it alone, try as one might. A *shared* understanding is required but can also be difficult to establish and readily undone. Coop-erative people will often agree about tolerance in the abstract but disagree sharply about tolerance in the specifics; they'll disagree about what is tolerable and where to draw lines. In the gray areas where the asshole flourishes, there aren't necessarily clear-cut wrongs, or, where the wrongs are clear, there aren't necessarily clear-cut sanctions to be applied. There may be no bright-line violation of reasonable expectations, and so ample room for dispute about what is or is not a genuine breach. There may be no clear and firm enforcement strategy, and so disputes may arise about what response, if any, to take. And there may be no obvious way to resolve these disputes. The disputes will center on deeply personal feelings and slight differences in interpretation from different vantage points. And those very differences in feeling and interpretation may lead to disputes about how to resolve disputes (e.g., about what workplace or meeting rules to adopt). There may then be no obvious way to get organized, no salient "focal point" solution to the general problem, that stands out as the way forward together.

This will be true even or especially when all are deeply invested in the joint venture. In the start-up company that promises to soon make huge amounts of money, few will be inclined to jump ship, even if staying on board means dealing with an asshole. Because the asshole requires the general cooperation of others to do his work, his extraction of special benefits from the relationship in effect exploits the participants' willingness to sustain it or, what comes to the same thing, their felt inability to leave. He cannot push too far, not so far that most involved decide that the burdens of asshole management just aren't worth it. But as long as the group remains persistently confused, the asshole can exert considerable influence over what the group does.

When a group does manage to arrive at a mutual understanding about asshole management, this will happen only because it has been graced with circumstances favorable for mutual understanding, which just as easily might not have happened. While success will usually have required a concerted joint effort, that is not to say that practice makes perfect, as it can in personal asshole management. Success is not a matter of personal devotion and time, since many different people must converge upon and work out a *common* way of getting on together.

Suppose, for example, that a group has finally hit upon a solution to its asshole problem. The conviviality of regular work parties (which the asshole does not attend) has restored a sense of common cause and created a way for the group to find shared solutions (a good idea circulates through the room). Consider why this might have happened. A few got into party planning and a few others came up with a few good, widely acceptable ideas. Yet that effort might easily have failed. The parties might not have caught on, or the asshole might have decided to attend, or the discussions might have reinforced or deepened the existing divisions.

Nor can it be generally assumed that, for each group afflicted by an asshole, there is some organizational strategy or other that will catch on if a few people just do a few of the right things. Asshole management is not prone to happen by itself, and it can be squelched despite great efforts. When success is a real possibility, this is so only because the stars align. Circumstances favorable for the group to work out their differences just *emerge*. Effort is not the better part of collective virtue, or even the half of it. Virtuous joint asshole management is in large part for fortune and fate to decide.

This needn't be reason to despair. It is, rather, all the more reason to uphold tolerance when it is, perchance, in our power, in cooperative good faith. It is all the more reason to stand ready to seek possibilities of cooperation when they present themselves, not to tolerate and appease the asshole but to tolerate one another and more forcefully resist him. Although there will usually be no "silver bullet" measure that keeps the wily asshole in line, and cooperative people will disagree about why a given management strategy fails and what to try next, tolerance will at least offer significant help in how cooperative people work out those differences and, in time, land upon an effective response.

Still, for all of our efforts, the asshole will in all likelihood never change. Should we despair in that fact? We argued in chapter 4 that he can be morally incorrigible and yet rightly blamed. Yet it is a further question how we should feel about and respond to the fact that even good management cannot be expected to bring him around, that we can *at most* expect him to be manageable, if even that. Are we then to ultimately write him off? The question raises the large issue of whether we can accept the givens of life that feel unacceptable, which we return to in chapter 7. Our answer will be this: we can at least still hope for the asshole's moral reform. That does not require expecting change as at all likely, and it is consistent with efforts at reform that do not fall into fruitless striving. The problem of the asshole is in this respect the problem of the human social condition generally. Reasonable hope is the key to acceptance, not only of the given asshole but of a social world in which assholes potentially flourish and abound.

This suggests that the problem of asshole management arises not simply in interpersonal relationships and in small groups but on a large scale. We now turn to develop that point in detail. As we will see, assholes threaten to destabilize whole societies, especially capitalist societies of the particular sort that we increasingly have.

[6] ASSHOLE CAPITALISM

⟨ Certain styles of capitalism are inherently prone to decline or, more specifically, to *degrade,* due to the proliferation of assholes. *Asshole capitalism,* as we hereby define the term, is the name of this kind of unstable social system.

Every kind of society requires a reliable asshole-dampening system—that is, a set of social institutions, such as the family, religion, public education, or the rule of law—that keeps the asshole population from getting out of hand. For if the proportion of assholes in the population becomes too large (i.e., the non-asshole to asshole ratio takes a dive), cooperative people will become increasingly unable or unwilling or just too few in number to uphold the practices and institutions needed for a society to stave off decline. If this is possible in any kind of society, asshole capitalism, as we will understand it, is *especially* prone to undoing itself in this way.

This is not necessarily to say that there is something about the very nature of capitalism that encourages people to be, become, or act like assholes.[1] That may well be true, and it

---

1. In general, a *capitalist* society widely relies on markets in the production and distribution of goods and services and in the allocation of capital. Instead of directing investment by centralized decision making, financial markets are trusted to put a society's savings to its most productive uses in the real economy. This general reliance on markets can take numerous different institutional forms, according to how market outcomes are or are not regulated and

does seem telling that quintessential capitalists such as John D. Rockefeller or Gordon Gekko are assholes.[2] But there are certainly assholes in totalitarian or socialist societies as well, such as Napoleon or any of the ruling pigs in Orwell's *Animal Farm* (recall the final commandment that "All animals are equal; but some animals are more equal than others"). Our argument in this chapter applies narrowly: it is addressed to capitalism in a particular, increasingly prevalent *entitlement-oriented style*. We will consider several ways a capitalist society might avoid this particular kind of entitlement culture and so avoid the asshole capitalism road to decline.

The asshole, as we defined him in chapter 1, feels entitled to special advantages of cooperative life to which he in fact has no moral claim. The culture of an asshole capitalist system, as we will understand it, sends just this kind of *strong entitlement message*. Roughly, the message is that you can rightly get something for nothing or get rich without having to worry about the costs to others. This message creates powerful incentives for asshole-style reasoning and action, not just among those who are already assholes but among many who would otherwise be content to cooperate as equals in society. The result is a profusion of assholery throughout social and economic life that overwhelms the dampening systems that might otherwise keep the asshole population from exploding out of control. As assholes grow in numbers, or are simply *perceived* to grow in numbers, cooperative people gradually withdraw from upholding the

according to what values. Our concern is with but one of innumerable ways of striking the market-state balance.

2. Though Rockefeller was also a great philanthropist. This mitigates against the asshole attitude reflected in his remark "God gave me my money."

practices and institutions needed for capitalism to function *by its own standards of value*. The capitalist system thus degrades: it becomes increasingly unable to fulfill its own promises of freedom, opportunity, and general prosperity, the very reasons cooperative people were supposed to want capitalism over other forms of society in the first place. In a word, asshole capitalism defeats capitalism's main point.

That is the main idea. To be more specific, asshole capitalism has three essential features:

(1) incentives: it affirms expansive entitlements (e.g., to unbounded personal enrichment, even at a social cost) that create powerful incentives for thinking like an asshole;

(2) undermanagement: it lacks a reliable system for dampening asshole profusion (e.g., the family or the rule of law is overpowered by the entitlement-based incentives); and

(3) destabilization: the resulting profusion of assholes undermines the cooperation needed for a capitalist system's healthy functioning, according to its own founding values (of freedom, opportunity, and general prosperity). The system, in that sense, deteriorates or degrades.

A helpful way to think about how this works is to start by imagining a capitalist society that more or less fulfills capitalism's social promises.[3] This means that cooperative people are, despite the usual assholes, mostly upholding the various

3. A more careful formulation of this idea is outlined in the Appendix.

practices and institutions needed for almost everyone to have things like real freedom, real opportunity, and a goodly share in general prosperity. But now suppose the society switches to an entitlement system (perhaps as the Entitlement Party rises to power). The system is now sending a powerful entitlement message, for instance, that having ever more is one's moral right, even when it comes at a cost to others. As asshole thinking and culture spread and take hold, the asshole-dampening systems that used to keep assholery in check become overwhelmed. Parents start preparing their kids for an asshole economy, the law is increasingly compromised, the political system is increasingly captured, and so on. As some switch sides while others mainly withdraw, cooperative people find it more difficult to uphold the practices and institutions needed for capitalism to do right by its own values. Although the society won't necessarily collapse—even assholes won't prosper if they take it that far—the practices and institutions that fulfilled capitalism's promises increasingly break down. The capitalist system, as we are putting it, degrades.

HOBBES BEATS MARX

Asshole capitalism, so described, is merely a disquieting possibility. It is a further question whether any real-world capitalist society, such as Japan, Italy, or the United States, should worry about the rise of asshole capitalism and its own decline. As we will elaborate later in this chapter, asshole capitalism is what social scientists call a "model," which will approximate reality only as a matter of degree. It is all-important not to mistake models for reality—however often professional economists do just that. Yet the important practical question is not whether we can be *sure* that the model is perfectly realistic but how confident we are that we are *not* already or soon to be on the road to decline the model describes. Our main task in this chapter will be to describe how a capitalist society may be undone. Our larger suggestion, however, is that we should be genuinely concerned about the capitalist societies we actually have. We should worry about whether our societies are already or might soon become asshole capitalist systems set on a potentially irreversible path of degradation and decline.

These things are difficult to estimate, but here is my own sense of the score, as of the early twenty-first century. Japan has little reason to worry, because its "collectivist" culture keeps people on a cooperative footing. Italy is already an asshole capitalist system and is contemplating routes of escape (the overdue ouster of Berlusconi being a start). The United States stands at the precipice: chances are fair to good that it has already reached a tipping point into asshole capitalism and perhaps irreversible decline. It could in theory return to its non-asshole capitalist glory days. But the shrewd gambler would not take that bet. Americans are therefore right to feel dread.

According to Karl Marx, capitalism is unstable but inevitably gives way to something better. The proliferation of assholes suggests that Marx was wrong: capitalism is unstable but can give way to something worse. Thomas Hobbes, that great student of the human condition, has a better nose for the asshole in human life. Hobbes argued that society was so inherently unstable that only an absolute monarch (such as the English king) could keep it from devolving into a "war of all against all," a hellish state in which, as Hobbes famously put it, "the life of man [is] solitary, poore, nasty, brutish, and short."[4] Hobbes

---

4. Thomas Hobbes, *Leviathan,* ed. Richard Tuck (Cambridge: Cambridge University Press, 1996), 89.

turned out to be wrong about the need for an absolute sovereign; the stable success of constitutional democracies with divided governmental powers, such as the United States and France, have proven as much. Yet the social dynamics of assholes may confirm his gloomy view of the risks. Cooperation is fragile. The prospects for any society depend to a large extent on circumstance and fate. And so cooperative people must remain vigilant if decent society is to last. Cooperative vigilance is the *only* bulwark against decline, *especially* in capitalist societies.

THE WAYS THINGS FALL APART: COLLAPSE, DETERIORATION, CRISIS, SYSTEMIC DYSFUNCTION

Social arrangements can come apart in various ways. Considering several of them will help to clarify the particular type of decline we mean to focus on.

Collapse. The now barren Easter Island once had a significant forest that sustained a vibrant society. The forest was gradually cut down, because each individual profited from cutting trees down but lacked assurance that if he or she didn't, others would likewise refrain. Largely as a result of this one "tragedy of the commons," the society died out.[5] Likewise, there's a fair chance that global warming will spell our collective doom (if not for all of humanity, then for vast numbers of people).

Deterioration. In other cases, we see degradation of something valuable without complete collapse. In one study of day care centers in Haifa, for example, fines were imposed upon parents who picked up their children late. As a result, tardy

---

5. Jared Diamond, *Collapse: How Societies Choose to Fail or Succeed* (New York: Viking Press, 2005).

pickups *doubled* (as compared with control groups). Moreover, they never returned to before-fine levels even after the fines were removed.[6] It seems the fine put people in a self-interested frame of mind (people were willing to pay for the extra time) that replaced a general sense of the obligations of cooperative child care. Or consider Richard Titmuss's famous study of blood donations. When people were paid to donate blood, overall donations declined. People were more strongly motivated to donate blood by charitable impulse than the profit motive. Here, too, market incentives displaced preexisting ethical commitment.[7]

There are also larger ways virtue can be "crowded out" by vice. The "crowding-out" effect in day care or blood donations can combine with the tendency for "markets to economize on virtue." The less markets depend on centralized decisions (about the allocation of resources, for instance), the less they depend on virtuous governors to make them. As Hayek puts it, the liberal market economy "is a system in which bad men can do least harm."[8] Taken together, the two tendencies can induce a mutually reinforcing downward spiral of market expansion and decreased reliance on virtue. As Samuel Bowles explains:

> The comparative advantage of markets over other institutions in governing interactions among self-interested

6. Uri Gneezy, "The W Effect of Incentives," University of Chicago Graduate School of Business, September 8, 2003.
7. Richard M. Titmuss, *The Gift Relationship: From Human Blood to Social Policy* (London: Allen & Unwin, 1970). For other examples, see Samuel Bowles, "Policies Designed for Self-Interested Citizens May Undermine 'The Moral Sentiments': Evidence from Economic Experiments," *Science* 320 (June 2008): 1605–9.
8. F. A. Hayek, *Individualism and Economic Order* (Chicago: University of Chicago Press, 1948), 11.

> actors [as set by decentralized decisions about relative costs, etc.] *may set in motion a spiral of market-induced erosion of other-regarding and ethical values, which in turn prompts greater reliance on markets, which in turn further erodes values, and so on.*[9]

We thus see a downward shift from a virtue-infused society to a more "virtue-efficient" end point.

Many have argued that this tendency is characteristic of capitalism and liberal institutions per se. Markets animated by self-interest, it is said, *depend for their very existence* on traditional familial or religious culture that encourages the personal and civic virtue needed for market-based society to work. And yet those same market relations *endanger* that very culture by displacing rooted ethical commitment with market values of self-interest. This, as the point is sometimes put, is the "cultural contradiction" of capitalism.[10]

Crisis. If these are cases in which something of value deteriorates, one could argue that the loss of value is nevertheless justified by gains for some greater value. Crises tend to be different in this regard: many crises do sweeping, irreparable, and largely unnecessary harm. Examples include a classic bank run or the global liquidity crisis of 2008. In both cases the destructive

9. Samuel Bowles, "Is Liberal Society a Parasite on Tradition?," *Philosophy and Public Affairs* 39 (2011): 46–81, italics mine. See also pp. 53–57 and Appendix 1 on p. 78. I am greatly indebted to Bowles's review of the issues and have followed many of his citations.

10. Daniel Bell, *The Cultural Contradictions of Capitalism* (New York: Basic Books, 1976). Similar themes have been sounded by Edmund Burke, Alexis de Tocqueville, F. A. Hayek, Karl Polanyi, Jürgen Habermas, Fred Hirsch, Joseph A. Schumpeter, and Robert D. Putnam.

outcome results mainly from *uncertainty* about whether loans will be repaid. Most parties were fine lending as long as enough other parties were lending as well. Without assurances that enough others are doing likewise, however, each faced an increased risk of default and so had a powerful reason not to lend or to recall debts. If there had been greater "confidence" that they would have been repaid, the crises could have been avoided, with little or no damage done.

Systemic Dysfunction. It is possible for a whole system to work in a way that repeatedly causes unnecessary destruction. The untoward outcomes are not simply a "forty-year flood" or "black swan event" but rather a predictable result of the way a system is set up and could be but isn't adjusted or reformed over time (if you like, a "white swan event"). Economist Hyman Minsky argued that capital markets are inherently prone to debt crises.[11] The tendency, however, is potentially manageable, and the development of central banking, for example, in fact dramatically reduced the crises that continuously befell unregulated private banks in an earlier era. Each era requires its own precautionary adaptations. In recent decades, however, we have mainly refused to take serious action. On a global scale, the Bretton Woods institutions adopted after World War II successfully limited and managed systemic risk for more than two decades; there were very few financial crises, not even a handful, before the system was abandoned in the early 1970s. But as capital became increasingly mobile across borders, as banking and investment were desegregated, and as confidence in laissez-faire rose (which allowed firms to make imprudent bets and shift risks off their balance sheets and so on), crises have

11. Hyman P. Minsky, *Stabilizing an Unstable Economy* (New Haven: Yale University Press, 1986).

increased dramatically in number and severity, culminating in the global crisis of 2008–9, the ensuing Great Recession, and crises in the euro zone.

CAPITALISM'S VALUES

Now compare asshole capitalism. It involves a kind of *deterioration* rather than complete collapse. The (perhaps gradual) process of deterioration results from *dysfunction* in the way things are set up or not adjusted and reformed. But this needn't be the result of a "cultural contradiction" with *traditional* values and the institutions and culture that instill them, such as the family or religion. As we will see, any and all dampening systems, traditional or otherwise, can be overwhelmed by the powerful incentives created by asshole capitalism's entitlement message.[12]

Our claim, specifically, is not that asshole capitalism leads to the end of capitalism or of society, but that it causes capitalism to take a degraded form, a form that is worse by *capitalism's own standards of value* than what came before. Does capitalism have standards of value?

Perhaps not, if you ask John D. Rockefeller. He'd presumably say that the point of capitalism is for him to get rich (or for God to have a way of giving him his riches).[13] Or perhaps he'd add something about the hardworking, risk-taking, exceedingly talented, ever-deserving, heroic entrepreneur. But we shouldn't ask an asshole what the point of capitalism is, since we can safely

12. For the social scientific case against seeing traditional family and culture as paramount, see Bowles, "Is Liberal Society a Parasite on Tradition?"

13. Which might even be consistent with Max Weber's famous account of how the Protestant work ethic supports capitalism by treating acquired wealth as a mark of salvation. See *The Protestant Ethic and the Spirit of Capitalism*, trans. Talcott Parsons (New York: Charles Scribner's Sons, 1958).

presume he'll simply advocate for asshole capitalism—at least assuming he's feeling sure he's in a good position to take advantage of it (and perhaps not otherwise). The value of capitalism is better settled by people who are not assholes, who have to do the work of upholding the practices and institutions needed for a functioning society, often at a cost to themselves. Why should they be willing to adopt capitalism instead of some other way of organizing economic and social life? The answer offered to us over the past two hundred or so years is that capitalism promises various desirable things, including freedom, opportunity, and general prosperity. It is supposed to advance the "general welfare" and create a "rising standard of living" in which "a rising tide lifts all boats," the yacht and dinghy alike. Capitalism, we have been told, advances these values as well as or better than alternative social forms.

Now, assuming for the sake of argument that this is right, it is extremely important that those grand promises can't be fulfilled without supportive social practices and institutions. The idea of a large-scale, self-sustaining, self-organizing "perfectly competitive" and "efficient" market is an intellectual fiction; it bears little relation to any actual real markets.[14] Large-scale exchange is possible, for example, only within a system of property that demarcates different things as "mine" and "thine." That will in turn require any institutions of security, law, contract, adjudication, taxation, and politics needed for the system of property

14. As the godfather of neoclassical economics, Nobel laureate Kenneth Arrow, puts the point, the proper functioning of markets depends on social and moral preferences. "Political and Economic Evaluation of Social Effects and Externalities," in *Frontiers of Quantitative Economics*, ed. Michael D. Intriligata (Amsterdam: North Holland, 1971), 3–23. For a similar point with emphasis on the practices or institutions that embed markets, see sociologist Karl Polanyi, *The Great Transformation* (Boston: Beacon Press, 1957).

to generally not fall apart (because of rampant theft or corruption or constant endemic conflict and so forth). If those practices and institutions aren't upheld, because cooperative people aren't willing to bear the cost of sustaining them, then the social promises of capitalism will not be fulfilled.

How might that failure look? In general, it might mean that living standards increasingly rise only for a fortunate few, that the "rising tide" of capitalism lifts the yacht but swamps the dinghy. The growth of gross domestic product year after year may increasingly become like everyone in a bar getting "richer," on average, because Bill Gates just walked in; average per capita wealth spikes, but most aren't personally richer for it. In more concrete terms, this might show up in various ways: maybe people become increasingly uncertain about their prospects for stable employment and eventual retirement, even though they have "worked hard and played by the rules" their whole lives; or perhaps people are increasingly unable to afford to stay in school, try as they may, because their increasingly vulnerable family needs them to work to pay urgent bills; or it could be that average people are increasingly unable to get the basic protections of law in an increasingly cash-strapped police or judicial system, even as the well heeled get the best justice money can buy; and maybe any or all of these trends result from political power being increasingly concentrated in the hands of an influential few, who steadily change the rules to further entrench that influence. In short, in one way or another, people increasingly see "liberty," "opportunity," or "prosperity" *in name only*, in a form that isn't especially valuable for them, that doesn't make good on the promise of capitalism in their eyes.

Here we should emphasize that we are not necessarily assuming deeper egalitarian ideas of social justice about how the outcomes of capitalism should be organized. I myself am a progressive in the style of John Rawls, which calls (roughly) for (1) equal basic liberties; (2) fair equality of opportunity in access to positions of greater reward and power, which dramatically mitigates the effects of fortunate birth; and (3) limits on the inequalities in income and wealth we allow in order to create incentives for hard work, risk taking, and so on, so that they must work out, over time, to the greatest advantage of the least well off social class.[15] But for present purposes, we can assume that no such requirements of justice apply. We assume *only* capitalism's own basic social promises. These do require advancing the *general* good but may not place any basic limits on the size of the gap between rich and poor. A yawning gap in wealth between richer and poorer might be problematic but for different reasons, say, because it means that too few are seeing real gains, because wealth is not being generally spread around, or because growth is not "broad based." Here we assume certain values but only *conservative* values. We assume only that we have reason to value the capitalist societies we have and so we have reason to prevent them from sliding into a degraded form.

Our remaining question, then, is how asshole capitalism makes things worse according to the values just described. Why, more specifically, would asshole capitalism devolve?

ENTITLEMENT CAPITALISM

Any capitalist system will create powerful incentives for personal enrichment. This is how it gets people to do things that

15. See John Rawls, *A Theory of Justice* (Cambridge, MA: Harvard University Press, 1971) and *Political Liberalism* (New York: Columbia University Press, 1993).

otherwise wouldn't be done. But the argument for a capitalist system needn't say anything more about such incentives, except that they do indeed work in getting people to do things that fulfill capitalism's larger social promises. Yet capitalist systems only work within a larger framework of social cooperation. So we should say some further things about the moral status of incentives and the conduct they induce. We should add, for instance, that people who respond to such incentives are potentially making a contribution, doing their part, and as a result do indeed have certain entitlements, for instance, to be paid what they were promised for services rendered or work done.

Crucially, this is not to say the entitlements are absolute. What one is entitled to, we may assume, is fair treatment by the system of social cooperation overall. Any specific entitlements one has are then subject to adjustment as needed for cooperation to be fair to all. So if the social promises of capitalism require increasing teacher or trash collector pay, then teachers and trash collectors will have a moral entitlement to a pay increase. And if those same promises include things like well-maintained roads and schools and refuse services, where this requires things like capping or heavily taxing banker or CEO bonuses, then bankers and CEOs have no moral entitlement against this change in the rules. All is fair if needed for capitalism to actually do what it is supposed to.

Now compare what we might call an *entitlement capitalist* system. Its very different message is of *basic expansive entitlements,* for instance, to an ever-greater share of the fruits of cooperation (e.g., parking spots, usable air, wealth), regardless of social rationale and regardless of what may be a significant social cost to others. Here we might think of bankers who profit from huge risks, knowing that their firms are "too big to fail" and that they will be bailed out in a crisis at the taxpayer's expense. Or, more pointedly, recall the dark fall days of 2008, when the U.S. and world economy was about to fall off a cliff, and U.S. treasury secretary Hank Paulson gathered the top bankers together to tell them that they were being forced to accept $125 billion, with no strings attached, in order to shore up their troubled balance sheets and buoy market confidence. To which John Thain, Merrill Lynch CEO, piped up and asked, "What kind of protections can you give us on changes in compensation policy?" This is a stunningly clueless asshole move. The taxpayers were in effect being forced, for the good of the country and the world, to protect the bankers from their own recklessness, at a huge cost. And yet the bankers' main concern was their *bonuses*.[16]

As this example suggests, the message of entitlement capitalism is of *expansive* entitlement (the bonuses are enormous). The message doesn't tell one to claim some specifiable share of goods, but rather that one can rightfully demand the *most* one can get, or at least *more* than others are getting, and certainly as much as or more than one got last time. One can't be expected to take a loss or even simply gain less for the sake of others. The message, moreover, is of *basic* entitlement, in the sense that one is entitled to ever more even when this has no further justification in terms of larger social purpose and perhaps despite significant costs for others. Because the entitlement is basic, no further such justification is required. Those who accept the entitlement message will of course cite platitudes that look a lot like further justifications—for instance, about the special role of people in their position (e.g., as "job creators," the "best and

16. Ron Suskind, *Confidence Men: Wall Street, Washington, and the Education of a President* (New York: HarperCollins, 2011), 123–24.

the brightest," "savvy businessmen," or "tops in their field"). But these are invoked more to bolster their moral confidence and silence those who complain rather than to open an honest discussion about whether the proposed benefits really are justified. Here moral confidence derives not from the merits of particular arguments but from the basic sense of entitlement itself. The sense of entitlement explains why those who have it are disposed to indignantly and aggressively defend it ever more as their right.

Our model here is the asshole as defined in chapter 1. He expects and demands entitlements to special advantages that he does not in fact have and yet is immunized against others who try to point this out. It is generally for morality to decide what one is or is not entitled to, and people of course disagree about what morality allows or requires. But for present purposes, we will assume, if only for the sake of argument, that one's moral entitlements are not expansive in the present sense. They are instead sensitive to what is required for capitalism to fulfill its social promises. Thus the culture of entitlement capitalism tells people they have entitlements that they do not in fact have.

Now, as we understand entitlement capitalism, the encouraged sense of entitlement is not limited to proper assholes. They do readily take to the message, since it confirms what they already believe about themselves. More important is that others who would not otherwise think like assholes are also swayed, especially as the entitlement message catches on. They, too, begin to *aggressively and indignantly* defend laws and institutions that give them an ever-greater slice of the pie, regardless of its social rationale and even at great cost to others. That doesn't mean assholery pervades all areas of life. The thinking may be limited to work or to politics, or generally to the economic system. (A society won't degrade even if asshole surfers proliferate out of control.) No one person need be very "systematic" across various areas of his or her life, and no one person need be particularly "entrenched" in this mentality. When the winds of culture blow in a different, perhaps more cooperative direction, many would go with the flow and perhaps later feel puzzled about how they could have previously thought so much like an asshole.

At issue, then, is a kind of culturally induced asshole moral *reasoning*. The reasoning may be expressed as a general *refusal* to think from behind John Rawls's "veil of ignorance." In asking what major social institutions would be just, Rawls suggests that we are to consider what kind of society we would be willing to live in, assuming that we are ignorant of our particular social position, including such things as our race, gender, class, or talents. The just society is the one we would each accept from this impartial point of view.[17] But because asshole reasoning tells a person that he or she is fundamentally special, this impartial perspective is either rejected or readily qualified. It is rejected or qualified on the basis of further specific entitlement claims that one wouldn't invoke without knowing what one's actual positions and prospects were like.

Since accepting the entitlement message is mainly *a way of thinking*, notice that it does not matter that not everyone can actually *have* ever more—except in a fantasy world of infinite economic growth and unlimited natural resources. For it is possible to have a fully *general* message of special entitlement in which each presumes that *others* will rightly bear the cost of

17. Rawls, *A Theory of Justice*, sec. 24.

one's benefit. In theory, everyone can *presume* that they have special status, even if not everyone can, in reality, receive presumed special benefits. All that follows is that some will be sorely disappointed and probably deeply upset.

Still, asshole reasoning will have some sense of limits. Even proper assholes will not knowingly push things into complete collapse. Where cooperation doesn't exist, as in Hobbes's state of nature, there are no special advantages for the asshole to take. Yet the asshole is perhaps not as careful as Hobbes's Foole, the cunning cheater who sees his share as optimized by keeping his cheating quiet so that he won't be caught and so it won't catch on.[18] The asshole is out in the open about allowing himself special advantages because he feels morally entitled to them. If collapse occurs as a result of assholes, it is only because assholes have mistakenly presumed that cooperative people would not become fed up and completely withdraw from cooperative life in any of the several ways we will explain. Still, because assholes do feel entitled to more, they are more likely to push it, and so are more systemically dangerous than the cautious egotist.

For purposes of our overall argument, the crucial feature of entitlement capitalism is that it magnifies the motivational power the incentives that already powerfully motivate people in a capitalist system. Things such as personal enrichment come to be seen as not simply attractive but as among one's basic rights. One comes to own those benefits as one's own in

18. Hobbes's reply is in effect that this will not work. David Gauthier's similar argument in *Morals by Agreement* (Oxford: Oxford University Press, 1986) is that people motivated only by self-interest will be unable to deceive others about their self-interested motives and so unable to earn the trust required for mutually beneficial cooperation. They therefore have to actually acquire moral motives in order to advance their overall self-interest. The asshole, by contrast, is morally motivated already.

an absolutist sense, quite aside from what fairness requires in the system of cooperation through which those benefits are created. It is this that gives entitlement capitalism an especially strong tendency to undo itself. Society becomes awash with people who are defensively unwilling to accept the burdens of cooperative life, out of a righteous sense that they deserve ever more. The entitlement style of capitalism is thus especially in need of strong correctives against asshole profusion. And yet that very entitlement ethos undermines the dampening systems that would otherwise keep assholes at bay.

OPENING THE FLOODGATES

We should consider in detail how this works. Let us assume for the moment that the encouraged sense of entitlement goes unchecked by any asshole-dampening system. The first question to ask is how assholes, unimpeded, might swamp cooperative life.

We said earlier that capitalism could fulfill its social promises only by way of various enabling social practices and institutions. But any such cooperative relations will be maintained in a population only because enough people each do enough to uphold the set of practices or institutions, at some cost to themselves. Enough citizens mostly abide by the law, pay their taxes, contribute to public goods, and so on. But, as we now explain, for any of several reasons, the spread of asshole culture in a system of entitlement capitalism can readily mean that not enough people are any longer willing or able to uphold social institutions and practices, including the institutions and practices needed for the capitalist system to live up to its own values. This may come to pass for any or all of a number of reasons, which we consider in turn.

SWITCHING. It may be that enough cooperators see assholes are doing better than they are. So they switch sides. "If you can't beat 'em, join 'em," they say. Moreover, the payoff for switching sides can increase as more and more people switch, much as the benefit of social networking increases as more and more people join a network. In that case, a switching trend will accelerate once it takes hold.

WITHDRAWAL. Many people will be resolutely antiasshole, however the cultural winds blow and regardless of the potential upside. Yet they may nevertheless find themselves unable or unwilling to maintain full cooperation. Instead of switching, they simply withdraw, being unable or unwilling any longer to do the things people need to do if cooperation is to continue as before. Withdrawal may take any or all of the following forms.

Exhaustion. Try as they might, in seeing assholes flourish, some cooperators will simply lose the motivational steam to carry on as before, perhaps while continuing to sincerely believe in the organizing values.[19] Steady, ongoing motivation may require a certain felt esprit de corps that was once there but has since fizzled out (whether by neglect or by sabotage).

Underassurance. It may instead be that everyone would easily and happily continue to do his or her full part, but only as long as each one can be assured that enough others are doing their parts as well. As each increasingly senses that others aren't pulling their weight, it will increasingly seem pointless to continue to do one's own part. Indeed, even if most people *are* in fact pulling their weight, the general *perception* that enough aren't can mean that not enough people will maintain cooperation going forward. The (mistaken) perception might result from seeing

---

19. Rawls calls this the "strains of commitment" in *A Theory of Justice,* sec. 29.

so many assholes on TV, from so many honest but unfortunate mistakes, from confusion or misinformation, or from a disinformation campaign led by assholes who profit when cooperative people withdraw.

Rising costs. In other cases, while the values advanced by cooperation previously seemed worth the personal cost to each of the cooperators involved, many have come to feel that the personal cost is becoming too high relative to the values advanced. Commitment might be strained or simply seem too high in principled terms (either because costs dramatically spike or because lesser value is assigned to the general values advanced). If enough people withdraw, then others who are willing to accept the higher costs may nevertheless find it pointless to be fully engaged for lack of assurance that enough others are doing likewise.

Unfair burdens. In other cases, increasing costs seem unfair. Even when everyone regards the overall costs of cooperation as justified by the values advanced, most will insist that the burdens of upholding cooperation be more or less fairly distributed if they or others are to be expected to continue to do their parts. If for some reason an unfair burden is placed upon enough people, they may become unwilling to carry on as before. When enough people feel so aggrieved and withdraw, others who feel more or less fairly treated may no longer see the point in picking up the cooperative slack or may feel that the new burdens are unfair to them.[20]

---

20. In still different cases, withdrawal may be a form of protest against gross and fundamental unfairness. Tommie Shelby defends this view of ghettoized black Americans in "Justice, Work, and the Ghetto Poor," in *Law & Ethics of Human Rights* (forthcoming).

So there are various ways cooperative life might deteriorate in the absence of a reliable curb on asshole profusion. How quickly this occurs depends to a large extent on prevailing social circumstances. An "external shock" to the system (e.g., a natural disaster, a war, a bond market crisis) can rally the cooperative troops and stave off or postpone deterioration. It may also mean only that the process of degradation takes a bit more time. (The process could be ineluctable precisely because each further degraded stage becomes the "new normal" and so fails to rally cooperative people.) Decline can also proceed relatively quickly, if not over a mere few years, then perhaps over a couple of decades. How quickly and in exactly what ways again depend upon circumstantial factors. The pace will increase when there is much to be gained from being an asshole or switching to asshole ways (e.g., when millions of dollars in pay are in the cards, as with big banks in recent years) or when cooperators are easily discouraged. An especially patriotic society might put up a long fight, while a society sharply divided in political outlooks might easily give up.

WHEN DAMPENING SYSTEMS FAIL

Now, even if a system creates powerful forces of asshole production, all is not necessarily lost: a reliable asshole-dampening system could in theory keep cooperative people assured that the proportion of assholes in the population is under some modicum of control. Enough cooperative people could then keep faith that enough other people are doing their parts so that the larger system of cooperation can be sustained. Not so in a system of entitlement capitalism. In this kind of system, as we are characterizing it, the powerful incentives equally undermine even the best mechanisms of asshole population control. These institutions, too, are eroded by the powerful incentives that entitlement capitalism feeds on.

Our remaining task in this chapter is to see how this might happen. We consider several of the main dampening systems in turn.

The Family. Loving family life encourages personal and civic virtue and therefore places some limits on net asshole output. In this the family is arguably indispensable. Yet that is not to say that it is sufficient *by itself* for asshole control. For the family is itself subject to the powerful tendencies generated within an entitlement capitalist system, and it needn't be entirely eroded to become ineffective as a bulwark against decline.

Consider how parents themselves might choose to raise their children in an asshole capitalist system. For one thing, asshole parents will tend to beget asshole children, compounding the problem. Even if they are merely assholes at work, this may still influence their parenting style; asshole bosses may be more likely to beget asshole children.[21] And among parents who are not in any sense assholes, they, too, may in effect be co-opted by the entitlement system. Parents often worry most about helping their kids make it in the system as it is, rather than raising them for a society that ought to be but might not materialize in the child's lifetime. So if there are powerful economic incentives for developing competitive dispositions (e.g., for jobs, degrees, or marriage partners), even well-meaning parents will often go

---

21. Apparently, parents who take orders at work put less value on independence in raising their kids, according to Melvin Kohn et al., "Position in the Class Structure and Psychological Functioning in the U.S., Japan, and Poland," *American Journal of Sociology* 95 (January 1990): 964–1008. The reverse tendency might also hold: parents who give orders at work may put greater value on independence in raising their children.

along with or encourage this, perhaps without appreciating that their children are more disposed to become assholes, or act like assholes, only after they leave the nest. If the rewards are great enough, many will seize the opportunity—perhaps in order to impress their parents with a large paycheck.

Nor is there an easy fix to this parenting predicament. The current trend of catering to a child's self-esteem by sharply limiting the experience of criticism or setback may encourage narcissism and only worsen net asshole production. Yet more traditional parenting methods may fare scarcely better. According to the spanking theory of virtue, for example, spanking is essential for teaching kids respect, and it is the turn against spanking that explains why there are more assholes than there used to be.[22] Quite aside from the morality of beating a child, however, spanking could well undermine a child's sense of fairness and personal integrity, in a way that facilitates his or her mistreatment of others, and thus provides little or no help as a dampening system. Even if it can in principle be done in the right way, we can hardly expect that at a societal level. Nor would homeschooling, say, underwrite the spread of civic virtue. It is clearly not feasible for a whole society, especially for families with working parents, and in any case everything will depend on the parents in question. If they gauge what is best for their child according to the powerful incentives of larger societal life, they may reinforce rather than correct assholish dispositions, as already suggested.

Religion. One might suggest that all this only shows that the

---

22. This theory was advocated (in personal communication) by sixty-five-year-old surfer Bob Montgomery, who pointedly claims that liberals and professors (like me, he notes) undermined spanking practice and thus caused the rise of assholes we see today.

family must work in conjunction with the socializing role of a religious community. That is no doubt helpful. But, again, the question is whether even the family and religion could provide a reliable bulwark against assholery when the larger economic system is creating powerful competing incentives. Family and religious institutions need only be substantially shaped by those incentives for assholes to gradually prevail. This can readily occur. Evangelical Christianity, for example, is one of the fastest-growing religions but also especially amenable to capitalism in an entitlement style. There's no reason to think that asshole capitalists do not regularly attend church. If a relatively few churches are uncomfortable for them, they can easily shop around for a church where their prowess in the market is prized and indeed regarded as a sign of God's blessing.[23]

Punishment. Even if we set spanking aside, threats of punishment do in some cases stabilize cooperation. Hobbes famously explained that the general threat of coercion by the sovereign gives each of us needed assurance that enough others will comply with the law. Even in some smaller-scale social relationships, cooperation can break down unless a threat of punishment is in the cards.[24] Could some system of punishment then be the key to asshole control?

23. Joel Osteen, pastor of Houston's Lakewood Church, one of the largest evangelical congregations in the country, goes one step further in his televised sermons, suggesting that if there were, say, two insurance agents in town and one of them committed to Christ while the other did not, then God would sluice more business the Christ guy's way. Osteen thus harnesses the power of the market in the service of religious entrepreneurialism. Apparently, God doesn't mind if faith arises from a profit motive.

24. This happens in some experimental games in which students are asked to contribute to public goods. See Bowles, "Is Liberal Society a Parasite on Tradition?," 67.

Probably not. What is distinctive about the asshole, in contrast with the outlaw, is that he is most effective in the gray areas, where violations of a social rule are difficult to establish in the public way needed to support unified efforts at social sanction. As we have seen in chapter 5, assholes often effectively turn cooperative people against one another precisely when agreement in such efforts is most needed. And even if sanctions could be established in some cases, it is not clear that any sanctions could apply in the general way that would be needed to keep the asshole population from getting out of hand. Indeed, in some cases punishment has the opposite effect of inducing vice. In some experimental "trust games," for instance, the threat of a fine imposed upon a player who does not sufficiently reciprocate a benefit received *reduced* the players' willingness to participate. Much as with the Haifa day care center, the fine put people in a self-interested frame of mind.[25]

Shame. An exception might be shame culture, which does seem to stably suppress assholery on a large scale in places such as Japan. Where that culture is not established, however, it is not clear what form of shaming could have a similarly general suppressing role. The media could potentially do so, and in some times and places they perhaps have. Yet the media is readily co-opted, perhaps more so than the family and religion. Consider Mussolini's or Berlusconi's Italy. Or witness the United States today, where an asshole parade in politics, cable news, and reality TV mainly reinforces a culture of shamelessness.

Liberal society. We might instead look to the institutions of liberal society (in the broad sense of "liberal" that contrasts

25. Bowles, "Is Liberal Society a Parasite on Tradition?," 60.

with authoritarian styles of rule). Institutions such as the market and the rule of law do apparently have a positive influence on civic culture.[26] Much as with the family and religion, however, the positive influence of such institutions can equally be undermined by the strong tendencies of entitlement capitalism. To the extent the rule of law involves effective threats of punishment, we have already suggested how it might be eroded as assholes avoid social sanction. And any positive influence on virtue induced by market relations might cease or be swamped by a more powerful sense of entitlement. Nor do the institutions of democracy provide a safe harbor. Electoral politics, as we all know, is all too easily corrupted. Even after the election, parliamentary rules are easily subverted for short-term political advantage.[27]

Perceived fairness. People reared in what they see as a fair system of cooperation arguably will do what it takes to support it. This may genuinely stabilize cooperation over time, from one generation to the next, if we assume a fair society has already

26. In numerous experiments, exposure to markets was correlated with and possibly a cause of support for liberal values (see Bowles, "Is Liberal Society a Parasite on Tradition?," 62–73). In experiments designed to measure a preference for fairness, groups that were more exposed to markets showed a greater generosity than control groups. In other experiments that measured willingness to contribute to public goods, participants from richer countries tended to contribute more for longer than in less market-oriented countries. Willingness to contribute also coincided with societies that scored higher according to measures for the rule of law, democracy, individualism, societal equality, and trust.

27. George Packer, in "The Empty Chamber: Just How Broken Is the Senate?," explains: "Like investment bankers on Wall Street, senators these days direct much of their creative energy toward the manipulation of arcane rules and loopholes, scoring short-term successes while magnifying their institution's broader dysfunction." *The New Yorker,* August 9, 2010, www.newyorker.com/reporting/2010/08/09/100809fa_fact_packer#ixzz1emqi5el2.

been established.[28] Even a capitalist society that is not seen as perfectly fair might garner its own support to the extent that each feels better off for it and is treated fairly enough. Still, this won't clearly help an entitlement system of capitalism. It loses support among cooperative people precisely because it is perceived as insufficiently beneficial and fair. At most, the sense of fairness might slow the process of decline.

Cooperative faith. A further possibility is that enough of us place our trust not in any particular dampening system but in our fellow cooperators as such. Despite perhaps yawning differences, we hold faith that they, like us, will do what it takes to keep things from completely falling apart. Yet, if this may well work under favorable circumstances, it surely has its limits. When circumstances turn unfavorable, even generalized trust can be shaken, for any of the reasons noted above (e.g., exhaustion, underassurance, rising costs, or unfair burdens). Societies once marked by trust do, after all, fall apart.

We have presented the possibility of decline in general terms. How or to what extent such dampening systems break down will vary from society to society, in part depending on how far entitlement culture has taken hold. I have suggested my sense of where things stand in a few cases (Japan is fine, Italy already qualifies as an asshole capitalist system, and the United States is in trouble). While I have my favored set of policy responses, our present point is more general: the risks to many capitalist societies are grave indeed. And even as constructive and potentially major solutions are urgently needed, there is no ready set of fixes. Much as with asshole management generally, as characterized in chapter 5, any degree of success will depend

28. This is the main idea behind Rawls's conception of stability in *A Theory of Justice*, sec. 69.

on both fortunate circumstances and the persistent efforts of cooperative people, made in good faith. The problem of the asshole, in this regard, is thus not simply a problem for capitalism, whether in entitlement-oriented styles or generally. As we will now see in the closing chapter of this book, the problem is, in a basic way, the problem of the human social condition itself.

[7] ACCEPTING THE GIVEN

❡ Assholes are a given fact of life. They are a fact of life we must somehow make peace with if we are to be at peace with life itself.

In one of his last published writings, the late G. A. Cohen, the brilliant and sadly missed political philosopher, begins with the following "Hegelian prelude":

> For me, it is a pregnant moment in the New Testament when Jesus, awaiting his arrest in the Garden of Gethsemane and foreseeing the toils to come, cries out "Oh, Lord, take away this cup," but then corrects himself: "but not my will, Lord, thine." The motif is abandonment of striving, of seeking a better state, and instead going with the flow, as do the lilies of the field, which are at peace with the world, and therefore with themselves.[1]

Cohen connects this with Hegel's obscure claim that "Spirit" achieves freedom when the subject finds itself in its own object, so that "it is home with itself in its own otherness as such." In plainer language: in accepting what is given, what is just there,

---

1. G. A. Cohen, "Rescuing Conservativism: A Defense of Existing Value," in *Reasons and Recognition: Essays on the Philosophy of T. M. Scanlon*, ed. R. Jay Wallace, Rahul Kumar, and Samuel Freeman (New York: Oxford University Press, 2011), 203.

we can, like the lilies of the field, be at peace with our world and so with ourselves.

Given our argument so far, it may easily seem that peace is impossible. Assholes are a given fact of life. They are not only a given part of each human's condition, in that few of us can wholly avoid interacting with them or expect them to change, but also part of the human condition generally. To different degrees in different eras and places, they are an unavoidable part of social life itself. Any attempt to eliminate them entirely would either fail or amount to tyranny.[2] But we have also said that assholes are unacceptable. We can't, or shouldn't, accept the way they treat us, even if we could get used to it. And we can't, or shouldn't, accept their destabilizing influence in cooperative life. Both are unacceptable from a moral point of view. This leaves us with a predicament. If peace depends on accepting the given, and assholes are a given fact of life, but assholes are also unacceptable, then being at peace seems to require *accepting the unacceptable*. To the extent that this is impossible or unjustified, so also is peace.

In this closing chapter, we explore a promising answer: there is a way of accepting life while finding much morally unacceptable about it. Hegel called it being "reconciled" to the human social condition. The question, then, is whether we can reconcile ourselves to a world of assholes. Can we be at peace with life despite the fact that assholes so often spoil it? Our answer is that we can, or at least that there is a decent argument for it.

---

2. How would the attempt work? Would we adopt asshole three-strikes laws? If you swerve through three lanes in traffic, park in the handicapped zone, and speak rudely to the coffee shop barista, you get ten years in jail plus time in an asshole reeducation camp. But would we not invariably sweep up innocent non-asshole jerks or pricks in the enforcement juggernaut? And would not assholes take over the asshole witch hunt?

Not only do we have reason to respect many of life's givens, but the human condition leaves room for reasonable hope for an acceptable social world. It leaves room for hope in part because the extent of asshole profusion is not simply given but to a considerable degree up to us, a matter of the kinds of societies we together choose.

STOIC ACCEPTANCE

As we might recall from chapter 5, the Stoics recommended ready acceptance of what is beyond our control. To the extent that the problem of the asshole, in our personal and social lives, is beyond the scope of our personal powers, we should simply accept it for what it is. Is this the way of peace?

The Stoics also made peace easy for themselves by allowing a kind of fudge: they insisted that the world is rationally ordered and in such a way that one could trust it to work things out for the best in the end. Likewise, Jesus in Gethsemane is not quite accepting the given brute facts of life and death but embracing a specific plan with a trusted cooperator, God the Father himself. It is quite a different proposition to accept the horrors of life, rank assholes and all, with no inkling of how they could somehow, even eventually, work out for anyone's ultimate good. If we do take the world to be rationally ordered, whether by Impersonal Rationality or by a Personal Divine Plan, then we are *not* accepting the given world as we know it, as it appears to our eyes. We are not making peace with *life itself,* but reconceiving "life" in terms that make it more acceptable than it would otherwise appear. We are holding faith that the world will somehow *become* acceptable in the end, not accepting the given world for what it just is—assholes and all.

When we do take seriously what the world really is like, Stoic acceptance becomes less appealing. Happy equanimity won't be appropriate when things become horrible enough to test any faith, when events and deeds cannot be plainly seen as part of any good and intelligent cosmic plan, and cannot clearly be justified by good things that might come from them later on. In a similar moment of existential despair, perhaps while thinking of Hobbes's "war of all against all," Kant writes: "If justice goes, there is no longer any value in human beings' living on the earth."[3] Writing with World War II in mind, Rawls elaborates the same dark thought this way: if a "reasonably just" social order is "not possible, and human beings are largely amoral, if not incurably cynical and self-centered, one might ask, with Kant, whether it is worthwhile for human beings to live on the earth."[4] If things get bad enough, because cooperative people have been thwarted at every turn, with no reasonable hope for a better state of affairs, it will be natural and reasonable to simply resign. We rightly won't settle for a world that falls so miserably short of our standards of how things ought to be or be made, even if that is largely beyond our personal control. The appropriate response is not Stoic "acceptance" but perhaps Masada-style mass suicide[5] or playing music as the ship goes down.[6]

If we have thus arrived at the problem of evil, the prob-

3. Immanuel Kant, "The Metaphysics of Morals," in *Practical Philosophy,* ed. and trans. Mary J. Gregor (Cambridge: Cambridge University Press, 1996), 473.

4. John Rawls, *The Law of Peoples* (Cambridge, MA: Harvard University Press, 1999), 128.

5. As in the ancient Hebrew mountaintop fortress of Masada, whose inhabitants chose dignified mass suicide instead of the murder, rape, and enslavement that would have ensued from an impending Roman invasion.

6. As portrayed, e.g., in the film *Titanic.* Nero fiddled as Rome burned, but presumably was in a position to do or have done something about it.

lem of the asshole is not quite so difficult. Even prospects of asshole-induced social decline are nothing like the moral threat to civilization presented by the rise of the Third Reich. Assholes do not usually prompt people to question the existence of a good and all-powerful God. Even so, the problem of the asshole is intractable in a special way. There is a lot to be done about grave evil, from law enforcement to war to reorganizing social relations in light of the great and existential threat. In World War II, the Allied powers were galvanized into action, knowing full well that the costs would be tremendous. After the war, the nations of the world took unprecedented steps to establish a framework for political and economic cooperation in hopes of lasting peace. These grand efforts, which largely succeeded, were facilitated by the salience of great evil and a ready consensus about its unacceptability. The problem of the asshole, by contrast, is marked by obscurity, uncertainty, and lack of easy consensus. As we saw in chapter 5, because assholes work in the gray, it is hard to know what to do or how far to go in asshole control. Cooperative people readily find themselves unable to muster the agreement and resources needed for an effective response. And after the well of goodwill has been poisoned, there is no easy way back to cooperative faith. Nor is the problem of the asshole limited to the occasional ruined afternoon or business meeting. It presents a major obstacle to progress and social justice but also threatens the hard-fought and hardwon gains for decency a society has already made. The problem affects whole societies, international relations, and so the entire world.

There is a second problem with Stoic acceptance, beyond the way it obscures the possibility of apt resignation in dire circumstances. It also stands in the way of the cooperative vigilance needed to prevent circumstances from becoming dire. One can accept that the world will always be imperfect, and that much of social life is not within one's personal control, and yet cooperate with others from a shared sense of the kind of society or business meeting that *we together ought to uphold*. That is not to deny the contingency of cooperation; fortune may to a large extent decide whether enough people can trust that enough others will not too easily resign. And cooperation will also depend on the vigilance of cooperative people in keeping faith with their fellows and refusing to resign, even against the odds. The abiding question of cooperative faith is what we can do together when each acts from our best common sense of what decency and justice require. But we will not effectively answer that question if we each happily give up on what happens to be beyond our personal powers in the Stoic style.

RESPECTING THE GIVEN

Fortunately, Stoic acceptance is not the only possible way of making peace with the human condition. As John Rawls develops Hegel's idea of "reconciliation," we can be reconciled to our condition, despite its evils, callousness, and unfairness, as long as we can credibly see the possibility of achieving a reasonably just social order. Reasonable hope for that possibility is all it takes for us to resist cynicism and temptations to resign. We can support efforts at reform that could, eventually, usher in a lasting peace.[7] As long as we can hold out hope for a significantly

---

7. These ideas are clearly present in Rawls's *The Law of Peoples,* but also in his *Political Liberalism* (New York: Columbia University Press, 1993) and, to a less evident degree, in his landmark *A Theory of Justice* (Cambridge, MA: Harvard University Press, 1971).

better, more just, and more peaceful world, we can be reconciled to our actual social condition long before a sufficiently improved state is reached and despite the fact that we may never see it in our lifetimes.

It is important that "reasonable hope" does not require *optimism* about the future. One might even be unwilling to bet against decline, because asshole profusion seems as likely as, or more likely than, not. Yet neither is reasonable hope mere wishful thinking. Wishful thinking does not require basic credibility, whereas *reasonable* hope depends on having good enough reason to support efforts toward reform over the longer haul. When reasons for hope aren't "good enough," resignation is justified.

While this is appealing, it cannot be the full story. If life were truly terrible, through and through, we could not be reconciled to it simply by virtue of the fact that there is an outside chance of significant eventual improvement, perhaps long after we (and our children, our children's children, and our children's children's children) are all dead. Reasonable but faint hope won't clearly suffice to stave off resignation in the face of an unacceptable and mostly bleak situation. Moreover, if there really were *nothing* to say in favor of our condition as it actually is, if there weren't some reasons to believe the given is in some sense a *good given,* then it would rightly be seen as little more than a giant *obstacle* to progress, a largely regrettable predicament. The ugly realities of social life—of moderate scarcity of resources, limited generosity, sharp limitations on understanding one another, and deep differences in outlook—will seem to do little more than make moral progress difficult, limited, halting, and slow.

We find help here in the idea that Cohen sees in Jesus' acceptance at Gethsemane: the idea that "we must accept some givens, not any and all givens, but plenty of givens . . . ," that "certain things are to be taken as they come: they are not to be shaped or controlled."[8] Cohen sees this as true conservatism.[9] This is not simply the idea that we are wise for accepting the limits of our powers, as though we would change things if we could, or even expand our powers, potentially without limit, if that were possible. Cohen does suggest that "we court vertigo if we seek to place everything within our control," but his point is not that, psychologically speaking, we simply can't handle it. It is that we shouldn't want to handle it, as a matter of value, even if we psychologically could, because "the attitude of universal mastery over everything is repugnant, and, at the limit, insane." He illustrates that repugnance with this allegory:

> Quite far along a certain continuum there sits a man who is surveying his own fleshly parts, that is, those of his parts which are *still* made of flesh, which includes some of his brain-flesh parts, and he is replacing defective bits of his flesh by perfect artificial substitutes, made out of whatever best serves, such as silicon, tungsten, reprocessed dung, and so forth. The man has been doing this for some time, and a lot of him is already artificial. That is surely a ghastly scenario.[10]

8. Cohen, "Rescuing Conservativism," 207–8.
9. Or rather one of three central elements of conservative conviction. The first is "a bias in favor of retaining what is of [intrinsic] value, even in the face of replacing it by something of greater value." The second is the personally valued. The third, which is our focus, is "the idea that some things must be accepted as *given* that not everything can, or should, be shaped to *our* aims and requirements; the attitude that goes with seeking to shape everything to *our* requirements both violates intrinsic value and contradicts our own spiritual requirements." Cohen, "Rescuing Conservatism," 207.
10. Cohen, "Rescuing Conservatism," 208.

The scenario is ghastly because, so we all believe, "certain things are to be accepted from nature, and that includes aspects of ourselves."

We might put the idea this way: much of what is given, including our fleshly nature, is, in a certain sense, *to be respected*. It is to be respected for what it just is, and therefore not to be wholly shaped or controlled (at least not without a pretty good justification). The body is not, then, the prison of the soul, as Plato thought, and the flesh is not to be resisted above all else, as for the neoplatonist Saint Augustine. Although the social body is not a fleshly thing, but rather made up of many different fleshly beings, it, too, is to be respected insofar as it is given to us, as are our basic forms of human relationship, human culture, and many of the social relations that assholes exploit: we are to respect those givens for the givens they are.[11]

That isn't to say we have to accept the ways we are *unjustly* treated by assholes, or the damage they do to given social relations. There is nothing in injustice or degradation to respect. Nor are we suggesting that respect for many of the givens of social life could reconcile us to the human condition all by itself; it still won't do if or when life is horrific. We still need reason-

11. Note that Cohen is Rawls's most famous critic from Rawls's left and that he means to challenge the "conservativism" of the present-day right as a perversion of its own conservative values. As he puts it, "For the sake of protecting and extending the powers of big wealth, big-C Conservatives regularly sacrifice the small-c conservativism that many of them genuinely cherish. They blather on (as Prime Minister John Major did) about warm beer and sturdy spinsters cycling to church and then they hand Wal-Mart the keys to the kingdom" ("Rescuing Conservativism," 225). The conventional ways of speaking of "liberal" and "conservative" outlooks, say, in England or the United States, have little meaning from a philosophical perspective.

able hope.[12] Our suggestion, then, is this: we can be reconciled
to our given condition insofar as we have reason to respect it for
what it is *and* reasonable hope that it can and will sufficiently
improve. That is a good and proper basis for refusing to resign,
for keeping faith.

CAN WE RECONCILE OURSELVES TO OUR WORLD OF ASSHOLES?

How does our world fare by that test? I leave a final verdict to
the reader. But here are some reasons why prospects for reconciliation are fairly good, despite the alarming and apparently
increasing number of assholes around.

For starters, there are our reasons to respect the many givens
of life, whether our fleshly existence or the basic sociability of
the human kind. We can add reasons why life can be beautiful
and good, as even the poorest of the poor will agree when they
gaze into their child's bright eyes. To the extent that life can also
be horrible, especially for the poorest of the poor, we can call
injustice what it is and work toward its rectification. If life for
many in our world is pretty good, the moral challenge is to make
it pretty good for everyone. We can labor to that end in reasonable hopes of this and other forms of moral progress, if not this
week, then not too far down the road.

In the bigger scheme of things, the arc of history does seem
bent toward justice, even as progress comes at an agonizingly

12. Rawls would happily accept the Cohen-inspired idea as a friendly amend-
ment. He might also agree that Cohen's conservativism supplies grounds for
rejecting a wealth-maximizing and fetishistic style of capitalism that both
Cohen and Rawls reject.

slow pace.[13] In the twentieth century alone we have the rise of democracy, the likely end to world war, the fortunate avoidance of nuclear holocaust, the rise of human rights discourse, and unprecedented gains in reducing absolute poverty. Here in the early twenty-first century, in the middle of the Great Recession, when this book is being written and when it will mainly be read, the future seems less than rosy. But the darkness was much darker not long ago, during the two world wars and the interwar and Great Depression years. While it may not happen very soon, the fog of crises eventually does lift, and there is room for hope (but perhaps no more than hope) that some lessons about the prudent management of financial markets will have been learned, or at least not forgotten too soon. There is at the moment little chance of immediate action to dramatically reduce the threat of catastrophic global climate change. Yet we can at least *hope* for a thaw in frozen political will. (Even as that may not happen in time to prevent collective doom, we can hope it happens in time.) Grounds for reasonable hope don't have to be conclusive or decisive. Reasonable hope, again, isn't predictive confidence.

13. Steven Pinker, in *The Better Angels of Our Nature: Why Violence Has Declined* (New York: Viking, 2011), argues that violence has markedly declined through history. Pinker suggests that the key to still less violence or greater peace is to use reason to seek not justice but peace itself, since people will disagree and perhaps go to war over their different views of justice. A major theme in Rawls's thought (e.g., in *The Law of Peoples*) is that a good measure of (nonretributive) social justice, duly sensitive to "reasonable pluralism," is a precondition for stable, lasting peace. People must feel they are being treated with sufficient fairness if their willing cooperation is to be sustained.

ROUSSEAU BEATS HOBBES

All of this will look like wishful thinking, like "utopianism" of
the bad kind, on bleaker views of human nature. We said in
chapter 6 that Hobbes was right and Marx wrong about the
fragility of cooperation and its progress. But Hobbes's explanation of the instability of society goes to the very impossibility
of human beings *ever* being brought very far beyond assholish
motives, given, as he puts it, a "generall inclination of all man-
kind, a perpetuall and restless desire of Power after power,
that ceaseth onely in Death."[14] People inherently seek to do
well for themselves by doing better than others. Fragile peace
among people locked in a relentless competition for relative
standing—for "vaine-glory," in Hobbes's term—is possible, if at
all, only with threats of sharp punishment meted out by a heavy,
authoritarian hand. If human nature is that bad, that fallen or
sinful in the religious idiom, then hope for progress is unreasonable: it just doesn't square with what we already know about
what people are like.

But are assholes really born and not made? Are they not
made by the society that deeply shapes them, as we have
suggested? Rousseau, our hero in chapter 1, argued, against
Hobbes, that our obsessive concern with relative standing over
others is not natural. Inflamed amour propre, as he called it,
is created by *society's* failure to recognize each as a full moral
and political equal. It forces people moved by their good and
natural sense of self-worth to seek recognition in established

14. Thomas Hobbes, *Leviathan,* ed. Richard Tuck (Cambridge: Cambridge
University Press, 1996), 70.

marks of relative standing—in being richer or smarter or hotter than their perceived peers. When society instead meets that need, people can be satisfied without having to be seen as *better* than others. They can sign on to cooperation with others, on fair terms that reflect the true moral equality of each and all.

In that case, even if a world without assholes isn't very likely, it is still fully consistent with the human social condition and so something we can reasonably hope for and work toward. Indeed, although Rousseau was content with speculative conjecture, which could be refuted by historical experience, history does seem to be working out as he hoped. As we have suggested, the rise of democracy, founded on the equality of each, has indeed coincided with a reduction in war.[15]

Hobbes's insight, which we developed in chapter 6, is that cooperative progress is not inevitable. The extent to which assholes pervade and undermine social life is to a large extent up to us. Assholes are produced by society, but society is ours to make and remake. So the acceptability of our social world is not a simple matter of accepting a given; it is ours to choose. We can together reject asshole capitalism and firmly resolve to move toward a more stable, more decent, and more just capitalist order, on a national and global scale.

To the extent we do not, it is because we have collectively chosen not to, not because we must accept and resign ourselves to a lesser fate. (Hence the paradox of Italy: it keeps bringing asshole capitalism onto itself. And yet we can hope that Berlusconi's ouster is the beginning of its end.) Although

---

15. This is Rawls's Rousseauian argument in *The Law of Peoples*.

we have emphasized that success in any such collective choice depends on fortunate circumstances, and that no one measure for asshole management could suffice, there is nevertheless much we can do to help ourselves along, to put ourselves in a position to get lucky, and together seize the moments of grace.

Those who are already cooperatively disposed can hold out in cooperative faith and adopt the attitudes that encourage it—attitudes such as tolerance, mutual understanding, and long-suffering. Those of us not yet cooperatively disposed will need a bit of help. Rousseau thus emphasized the paramount importance of moral education.[16] In most present-day societies, we aren't starting from scratch; the question is whether the institutions of moral learning can be sustained and improved. That will probably mean doubling down on public education, with more humanistic study and less economics (at least at the university level, where it has been shown to make people selfish). It will also probably mean improving religious culture. Catholics might be encouraged to regularly confess the sin of pride. Evangelicals might learn to be less selective in their concern for social justice. It could even mean teaching intelligent design in schools—albeit in philosophy courses rather than science class (which may need to be instituted). To the extent we are on the sinking asshole-capitalist ship, the tired culture wars (e.g., in the United States) are themselves a grave and gathering threat. The proper attitude is "all hands on deck."

―――――――

16. Especially in *Émile*.

If humanity had a body, it would have an asshole—namely, the asshole himself. Life invariably has a certain foulness, and he embodies it. All too often, fair is foul and foul is fair. Yet the witches of social life cannot foretell our fates. Social life can be fairer and less foul, if, but only if, cooperators of the world unite.

LETTER TO AN ASSHOLE

⁋ (*Written in the spirit of Horace's epistles: "Now therefore I lay aside both verses, and all other sportive matters; my study and inquiry is after what is true and fitting, and I am wholly engaged in this.*")[1]

My friend:

I write hoping to persuade you to change your basic way of being. I do not presume that you will come to agree with me that you do not have the entitlements you so often assume. Nothing I could say by way of pure reason can coerce you into accepting a view you are simply unwilling to hold. But I do at least want to offer some reasons why you might reconsider your firm stance. Ultimately, of course, you can take them or leave them. My hope is that you give them a hearing.

I'm sure you found my chapters quite unfair to you. I have written much about you without speaking to you directly. I claim you won't listen, but I have not given you a serious argument. I say you are mistaken but presume that reason supports my position. All of which must lead you to wonder about my motives. Do I think I have a serious argument or not? Instead of my soft, crowd-pleasing disputations, why won't I just

1. From "To Maecenas," *Works of Horace,* trans. C. Smart (London: Bell & Daldy, 1872), book 1, epistle 1.

make my case honestly and forthrightly? Am I too lazy, or too cowardly, to follow reason where it leads? Do I perhaps know and rightly fear that the weakness of my arguments will be exposed?

I take your point. So I address you here to give you my argument, an argument that you really *should* come to recognize others as equals, that you *should* in this way change your basic way of being.

I admit that I present my argument in writing in part for fear of speaking to you in person. When Kafka wrote to his father, he had plenty to say but feared that the right words would evade him under the glare of his father's supreme confidence. I, too, worry about getting a word in edgewise in person. But while Kafka hoped he and his father could each accept the other's innocence, I do not seek that way of making peace. I still maintain that, in the dispute between us, you are the one in the wrong. Even if you won't finally agree with me in this, I have, as you'll recall from chapter 7, made my own kind of peace with this, my own way of accepting as a given that you may never change.

As for why you would listen to me at all, my sense is that I might pique your curiosity. Might I actually understand your much misunderstood position? I have labored, in anger but also in sympathy, to appreciate your perspective. I even have a distant gratitude to you for all I have learned with an uneasy sense that, but by grace and fortune, I could easily be much the same as you. I am also well aware of the intellectual resources at your disposal. Having read Nietzsche, I know that "morality" can be seen as a device of the masses' wretched envy, of insecure pride expressed in moral language, as a flailing effort to subdue the few and the strong by the weak and the many. In that view of morality, which you might well agree with, you are the authentic moral hero, while my arguments only aid in the oppression of the great by the small. So I have a sense of what I am up against. Finally, I understand that there can be no refutation of the dug-in skeptic, who denies our knowledge of external things or of objective values. Descartes showed us the folly in expecting proof of human affairs as in mathematics, with its clear and distinct certainty. Reason is a gentler method, which one can decide not to hear. So, you might say, if the envious and unworthy masses will not see good reason to bow to true talent, to accord you the special treatment you in fact deserve, then what can be done about them? Why grant them a hearing at all?

Before I give you my own argument, you might find it of interest to remember the wise and chatty Horace, who shares your appreciation of superiority. He writes to Maecenas:

> The wise man's second only to Jupiter:
> He is a king of kings in his own life,
> As the Stoics say; free, beautiful, most honored,
> And above all else he's reasonable and sane,
> Unless, of course, he's got a bad toothache.[2]

You style yourself as the king of kings in your domain, but not simply because you *do* dominate others. You are *worthy* of ruling others, because you are their better. If so, you must not be like bad poets, of whom Horace says: "If they hear no praise from you, what do they care? / Deaf to your silence

2. This is from a translation I like especially well, that of David Ferry, *The Epistles of Horace* (New York: Farrar, Straus and Giroux, 2001), 11.

they'll praise themselves, serenely."³ You should be open to
wise counsel—if not from me, then maybe from Horace. "All
swollen up with love of glory, are you?" Horace offers ironic
reassurance:

> Nobody's so far gone in savagery—
> A slave of envy, wrath, lust, drunkenness, sloth—
> That he can't be civilized, if he'll only listen
> Patiently to the doctor's good advice.⁴

What might Horace recommend to you? First off, he might
suggest taking it easy. You are tense. You stand ever ready
to guard your special standing in a bold showing of how you
will not be questioned. That cannot be terribly comfortable.
And surely you do like to relax, to be at ease, alone or among
friends. With a friend, you sometimes grant him his point or
cut him slack if he makes a simple error. So why not extend
the courtesy to others, if you happened to commit the wrong?
Why not be the one who, this time, just admits the mistake,
instead of defending your innocence and convincing only
yourself? The admission can be quickly made and forgotten,
leaving you free for pleasant activities without stewing in hot
resentment. Horace and I agree: you should take a long, cold,
intelligent look at pleasure; it hurts you if you purchase it with
pain. The man whose anger gets out of hand will wish he
hadn't done the things he did to satisfy the hunger of his rage.
A fit of rage is a fit of honest-to-goodness madness.⁵
    You'll object that you do have sound reasons for being angry,

3. "To Julius Florus," *The Epistles of Horace,* 141.
4. "To Maecenas," *The Epistles of Horace,* 5.
5. "To Lollius Maximus," *The Epistles of Horace,* 17.

reasons that aren't about your pleasure or happiness. You are defending your sovereign liberty. Madness, you might say, is a small price to pay for the freedom to have what is rightfully yours.

But have you counted the cost of such freedom? Horace will point out that you are deciding what is rightfully yours by constantly comparing yourself to others. "When your neighbor grows fat, you grow thin."[6] And life is such that there is always someone to best, if not your supposed peers, then the best of the best of yesteryear. However fast you run, or however rich you become, there will always be somebody just out in front, whom you'll be anxious to get ahead of, or someone just behind, against whom you must keep your lead. Such is no doubt the way of the world. But that means, in effect, that you are following conventional wisdom, as Horace puts it:

"Fair means or foul, get money if you can;
No matter how you get it, be sure you get it"
—All for a seat down in front at some bad play?[7]

In which case, how can you truly be free? Are you not yourself a slave to the conventional status contest around which so much of society is run? As Horace says, anxiety owns the man who is owned by greed. He whom anxiety owns is therefore a slave.[8]

There's a lesson here: anything rightly called "sovereign liberty" begins in self-discipline. Horace recommends virtue. Let's start with yours. You pride yourself on your mental

6. To paraphrase from "To Lollius Maximus," *The Epistles of Horace*, 17.
7. "To Maecenas," *The Epistles of Horace*, 7.
8. "To Quinctius," *The Epistles of Horace*, 79.

faculties and fastidious habits, and you denounce the sloth and stupidity of the unemployed masses. But allow me to inform you of what any good friend would point out: most people find your very presence pretty unpleasant; your encounters leave a mental aftertaste much like an unpleasant aroma.

It would improve matters if you kept your inner disposition more hidden. You surely value modesty in others, because it creates a self-respecting public presence. So follow Horace's example, as when he tells Augustus why his poetry "keeps itself so close to the level ground":

> I know that I myself wouldn't relish being
> Acclaimed in some wrongheaded panegyric
> Or having my face, misshapen, portrayed in wax.
> This fatuous praise would make me blush with shame,
> As, with my praiser, the two of us together
> Are carried off, stretched out in a closed casket,
> Down to the street where cheap perfume is sold,
> Incense, pepper, spices, and all sorts of other
> Odoriferous things wrapped up in old waste paper.[9]

Fame and infamy are uncomfortably close. Modesty seems much the better strategy.

I suspect you are thinking that all of this reasoning is really not at the heart of the dispute between us, or at best is inconclusive. And you would have a point. There are deep philosophical reasons why you might take objection to the ancient marriage between morality and happiness that underlines my argument. Here Kant, who sharply divorced

9. "To Augustus," *The Epistles of Horace,* 131.

morality from happiness in the name of reason's own limits, oddly helps your position. When you say that you have your special entitlements and that I have special duties to you, you can maintain that it is simply a separate question entirely as to what makes either of us successful or shameful, happy or hated. First and foremost, our question is a moral one: Do you in fact have your assumed entitlements, from a purely moral perspective?

You will appreciate the irony in the idea that Kant, that great moral rigorist, would help the retrenchment in your position. No philosopher rejects your point of view more resolutely, and yet you can turn this to your dialectical advantage. Kant famously claims that we can, as rational creatures, appreciate the "fact of reason": we learn that we can in fact keep the moral law, because we sense, perhaps despite our willful resistance, that we ought to. You will happily admit that. You find the moral law deeply convincing and merely apply it in a way that gives you special privilege. When you become angry, you say that the moral law, as you apply it, is the basis for your objection: you are squarely within your rights and merely exacting the respect you truly deserve from others.

As mentioned in chapter 1, Kant seemed aware of your particular condition. He called it "self-conceit." The trouble is that you could easily regard this label as little more than name calling. Certainly the phrase itself does not explain why you are in error. Kant mainly insists that you are wrong. Following Rousseau, he writes that "we all have the right to demand of a man that he should not think himself superior."[10] But your

10. Immanuel Kant, "Proper Self-Respect," in *Lectures on Ethics,* trans. Louis Infield, with foreword by Lewis White Beck, (1963; repr., Methuen: London, 1979), 127.

question is *why* one ought to avoid self-conceit, and Kant does not seem to have a plain answer to that question.

What Kant does offer, by way of reply, is his pious praise of the moral law's purity, as though it will itself somehow lift you out of your condition: "The purity of the moral law should prevent him from falling into this pitfall, for no one who has the law explained to him in its absolute purity can be so foolish as to imagine that it is within his powers fully to comply with it."[11] But merely invoking the purity of the moral law will not move you, and you won't find any impetus for change in realizing that you can fall short of it. In your interpretation, you will admit that you occasionally fail to give yourself your due and that you can learn what your superiority entitles you to from others. Your question is still why this should be so wrong. And what Kant does say, finally, as an answer really does seem to be name calling: you are "pettifogger," who "grows deceitful and cheats about the facts," as little more than a "twister."[12] Indeed, he goes so far as to call you evil:

> There is nothing worse, nothing more abominable than the artifice that invents a false law to enable us, under the shelter of the true law, to do evil. A man who has transgressed against the moral law, but still recognizes it in its purity, can be improved because he still has a pure law before his eyes; but a man who has invented for himself a favorable and false law has a principle in his wickedness, and in his case we can hope for no improvement.[13]

11. Kant, "Proper Self-Respect," in *Lectures on Ethics,* 128
12. Kant, "Self-Love," in *Lectures on Ethics,* 137.
13. Kant, "Self-Love," in *Lectures on Ethics,* 137.

In short, Kant treats you like a psychopath when you are in fact not one. You raise a serious moral question, which we have yet to answer.

I hope this shows you that I appreciate the force of your position. I take it seriously. And yet I do think you can be answered. You are, I suggest, caught in a dilemma, which might be put as follows:

On the assumption that you are not just a psychopath, you must be able to justify your claim to special moral privilege. And that means you'll also have to accept a demand to offer basic, recognizable forms of moral justification. Otherwise, your claim of moral justifiability will be little more than a false pretext, a kind of sham. Our moral conversation is then over. You wouldn't really be defending your special status. You'd merely be acting like a psychopath. That is, you would be refusing to engage your own moral concepts by putting yourself beyond the reach of moral discussion.

On the other hand, if you seriously engage the question of how your presumed special standing could be justified from a moral perspective, then you put yourself in a weak and finally unsustainable moral position. You can keep a pretext of moral justifiability only by refusing to follow the moral argument. You are stuck making bad moral arguments defensively.

Let me elaborate. You are not a psychopath, again because you engage in and are moved by moral reasoning and not just in defense of your prerogatives. You would recoil with indignation if your wife were betrayed by her business partner. That is plainly a moral reaction. And you have felt the same way about others whom you've seen wronged, even others with whom you have no special relationship, such as the abused child in the neighborhood or the innocents needlessly killed in war. In one

degree or another, you feel some basic moral concern for everyone. Your view is that such people are less deserving than you
are but not that such people are owed nothing at all. Morality
is in a basic way about what is owed to everyone.

But now, to press you further, we should ask about the
nature of your own presumed special moral status. You are,
you say, a special case. We must ask why that should be so,
for reasons that do not wither under easy scrutiny. Here, I
claim, you are left with plainly bad arguments, arguments you
yourself would not accept unless you were resisting a line of
thought for fear of where it would lead. Specifically, because
you have moral notions of right and wrong, you must take the
bare fact that *you* are at issue to be morally irrelevant. There
must be reasons, which present your *situation* as different, that
can be properly evaluated in terms we can all understand and
accept. But this is precisely where your thinking gets
shoddy.

Notice the way you sometimes use the pronoun "I" in a
magical way. You used it so during our last lunch meeting,
when you said to the maître d', as regards our having to wait to
be seated, "Do you know who I am?" You assumed that anyone
would know that, somehow believing that a description of your
station would bring a special privilege of expedited seating.
The pronoun "I" won't itself indicate that special situation. It
means the same for anyone. It refers to the speaker who uses
it, who need only speak the language. In that regard, even the
masses are your equal. So, if there are reasons for the maître d'
to favor our being seated while others are waiting, there is, as I
say, no magic in the word "I" to indicate them. You must have
good reasons and be ready to produce them.

What would you say to justify this privilege? Perhaps you

might mention your important job. Yet the people waiting also have jobs and they no doubt think them important. So you'd have to explain what is special about your job in particular. Maybe you'd mention that you are very well paid. But that won't explain why you should not be asked to be kept waiting. For that, what you would have to tell us is that you are *underpaid*, that you need the benefit of expedited seating in order to make up for inadequate wages or for your tough day at the office or some such generally acceptable reason. Otherwise, if we consider your precise reasoning, it is hard to find a recognizably moral argument in what you are saying; you are then just asking to gain on the grounds that you've gained already. To make this argument out in the open, with others waiting, would demonstrate your moral incompetence. While I'm sure you could silence objections by asserting your claim confidently and loudly, it would not make your claim any more acceptable from anyone's perspective. It would not be morally justified.

This, I assert, is your awkward predicament for any and all of the various overstretched reasons you give for your distinct moral status. My first demurrals touched upon many of them with no attempt to settle the issue. But that was the start rather than the end of my argument. Presented systematically, they leave you only with shameful defenses. My guess is that you sense that your prospects are not especially good when the moral considerations are culled and carefully analyzed. Better, then, to stay on the defensive, to stop the argument before being exposed by it.

In at least one way, then, Horace and Kant may be kindred spirits after all. As I should have mentioned earlier, Kant likens self-conceit to a rock upon which "man is

wrecked."[14] Your awkward position makes things harder on
yourself than they need to be. It is strenuous to hide from
your own reason, to force your own mind away from the
direction it would most intelligently lead. What is more, and
worse, a person can be wrecked for being alienated from his
or her own deepest longings for the most valuable relations we
can have with others. We can see moral reasoning as a kind
of self-transcendence. It flows beyond your own experience,
bringing you out of your own perspective into the lives of others and to another side of reality. The reality has them and you
in it. You see yourself from their standpoint. They see themselves in yours. You together make a real unity. This mutual
perception grounds most human connection, and much of
what we value in any human relationship depends on our
suitability for such moral recognition.[15] But you make yourself
unsuitable for it.

   If that is right, then you face grave risks. If I may say so, as
you are, it is as though you sit, squatting, defiant, and starving,
in a dark cave of your own making. You prefer to be feared, if
not respected. In that way you strive for a pale copy of true
moral recognition. There is an easier way. But ease is hardly
the whole of it. I fear for you mortally. You will remember
Dickens's final premonition for Scrooge: that there would not
be "a man, a woman, or a child to say that he was kind to me

14. Kant, "Self-Love," in *Lectures on Ethics,* 128. You might have come across
Christine M. Korsgaard, *The Sources of Normativity,* ed. Onora O'Neill (Cambridge: Cambridge University Press, 1996), who develops the idea, on Kant's
behalf, as a way one's agency and very person disintegrate.
15. A nice explication of Sartre's account of this mutual perception can be
found in Thomas Nagel's "Sexual Perversion," in *Mortal Questions* (Cambridge: Cambridge University Press, 1979), 43–44.

in this or that, and for the memory of one kind word I will be kind to him."[16] In their hearts even the most generous souls would be thankful for his demise. It pains me to tell you that, just so, many who know you will find your death relieving. There will be a quiet celebration. I imagine you do care about that. You would not like the epitaph that I would write for you, for example. Or maybe you aren't bothered. Either way, please accept my honest concern for your health and safety. One could easily pity your condition, and so I hope you change it.

Sincerely yours,
A. J.

16. Charles Dickens, *A Christmas Carol* (London: Chapman and Hall, 1897). Available at the Electronic Text Center, University of Virginia Library, http://etext.virginia.edu/toc/modeng/public/DicChri.html.

ACKNOWLEDGMENTS

This book is inspired by surfers, especially the asshole surfers who reliably appear, with remarkable similarity (albeit with regional stylistic differences), at the main surf breaks around the world. Although our global tribe is hardly special (academia, my other tribe, also has plenty of assholes), I owe a special debt of gratitude to my fellow surfer tribesmen who have proven, over many years, to be a rich source of both irritation and intellectual stimulation.

My basic definition of the asshole was originally formulated at the beach, with the help of four friends from the University of Manchester Surf Club, during their summer visit from England in 2008: Danielle Bjelic, Rich Claughton, Tim Quick, and Lucy Thompson. The theory was further enriched by numerous inter-disciplinary conversations over lunch during my fellowship year, 2009–10, at the Center for Advanced Study in the Behavioral Sciences (CASBS), Stanford University. A first short version of the theory was drafted at the center on a brief break from my normal research on fairness in the global economy, which became a book entitled *Fairness in Practice: A Social Contract for a Global Economy* (New York: Oxford University Press, 2012). The initial short draft was considerably revised with the wise guidance and support of Donald Lamm. Without Don, the book would not have happened; the ideas would have remained a way of blowing off steam. I am also grateful to Melissa Chinchillo, who, with Don, guided the project, placing it in the hands of Gerry Howard, by all accounts (and especially mine) the very best editor this project could have had.

The book is the product of many minds and many enjoyable conversations. For regular exchanges and encouragement, I especially thank Taylor Blodgett, Marshall Cohen, Margaret Gilbert, Sunny Karnani, and David Tannenbaum, with special thanks to Fiona Hill and Nicholas Jolley for discussion of public and historical figures, and to Cristiana Sogno for suggesting a Horatian version of the Letter to an Asshole. I am indebted to John-Paul Carvalho and Jennifer Herrera for help with the game theory appendix, and to the UC Irvine graduate students in our asshole discussion group at the Anteater Tavern, which included Andreas Christiansen, Michael Duncan, Matthew Dworkin, Justin Harvey, Violet McKeon, Daniel Pilchman, Valentina Ricci, Justin Thomsen, and Amanda Trefethen. For their insights, I also thank Secil Artan; Graeme Bird and Kerstin Maas; Xavier Cornillie; John Dent; Joseph Dowd; Ed Feuer; Luca Ferrero; Steve Finlay; Mark Fiocco; Al Franklin; Samuel Freeman; Julia Fremon; Brad Frohling; Nathan Fulton; Mike Granieri; Sean Greenberg; Phil Goodrich; Liz Harman; Nicole Hassoun; Matt Hayden; Jeffrey Helmreich, Pamela Hieronymi; Kristin Huerth; Nadeem Hussain; Linda Jack, Alex, Alin, Elizabeth, and Wendy James; Thijis Janssen; Mark Johnson; Melissa Johnson; A. J. Julius; Ken Keen; Erin Kelly; Bonnie Kent; Louise Kleszyk; Rahul Kumar; Doug Lavin; Brian Leiter; Alissa Maitino; Daniel McClure; Dan Oberto; Alexi Patsaouras; Casey Perin; Cynthia Pilch; Jesse and Elaine Pike; David Plunkett; Mike Powe; Ankita Raturi; Andy Reath; Holly Richardson; Vanessa Rollier; Jacob Ross; Chris Sanita; Debra Satz; Lucy Scanlon; T. M. Scanlon; Ricky Schaffer;

Tamar Schapiro; Martin Schwab; Bob Scott; Brian Skyrms; Kelly Slater; David W. Smith; Larry Solum; Lucho Soto; Eric Schwitzgebel; Dan Speak; David Sussman; Julie Tannenbaum; Paul Tannenbaum; Peter and Sally Tannenbaum; R. Jay Wallace; Leif Wenar; Stephen White; Douglas Woodward; Gideon Yaffe; the 2009–10 fellows at CASBS; and the audience at a CASBS continuing-studies lecture at Stanford University. I apologize to anyone I forgot to mention; the book is still better because we talked. Finally, I am grateful to Peet's coffee at the University Center in Irvine, California, where much of the book was drafted during the fall of 2011.

I share the reluctance about "pop philosophy" widely felt among professional philosophers, and it has been uncomfortable to relax (some might say abandon) the usual professional standards of rigor and decorum in favor of much tomfoolery. The risk of transgression, of doing bad work, and of forgoing important projects, even if temporarily, has seemed tolerable only given my hopes of offering a different kind of contribution: a book that shares all the fun conversations I've been having; that gives succor to those afflicted by an asshole; that offers a glimpse into philosophy through a basic human concern; and that draws together standard philosophical themes in a new way. I thank the many people who encouraged me in this. I also thank those who urged caution, for caring enough to say something.

A Game Theory Model of Asshole Capitalism

Our story of asshole capitalism's decline in chapter 6 is inspired by the formal theory of games. I therefore consulted Oxford-trained UC Irvine game theorist Jean-Paul Carvalho on how this distinctive process of decline might be modeled. Over a fruitful lunchtime discussion, Carvalho thought up and proved (with simple, mainly illustrative math) a possible model that captures central features of the way asshole capitalism undoes itself. This appendix describes the model for the general reader while providing some background explanation of game theory. (It was written with the generous help of talented UC Irvine logic and philosophy of science graduate student Jennifer Herrera.)

The theory of games studies how different agents would strategically interact, given the choices of other agents. Each player in the game is said to have preferences for how things go, which he or she acts on, depending on what other agents are choosing. The theorist considers what patterns of action emerge when such players interact, in a single round of play or in repeated interactions.

In the "stag hunt" game inspired by Rousseau, for example, each player—"you" and "I"—can either hunt stag or hunt hare. If we both hunt stag, we both eat more bounteously than if we each separately hunted hare. So we both prefer to hunt stag. However, both of us must join the hunt—we both must cooperate—in order for either of us to reap this greater benefit. But neither us can know whether the other will in fact show up for the hunt. If you show up and I don't, you miss out on a chance of hunting hare, or indeed of hunting at all, and wind up with nothing.

What should you do? Take a risk on the greater benefit of bounteous eating? Or play it safe and simply hunt hare on your own from the start? The answer depends on what you think I will do, how sure you are in that belief, and what risks you are willing to take. Hunting stag is obviously the best option for both of us, and it is perfectly possible. Nevertheless, the best course might not be taken, simply because of our uncertainty about what the other will do. If you are like most people, you won't pass up a modest but certain benefit for a better but uncertain possibility of gain, and so you'll choose to hunt hare on your own instead of taking a risk that I won't show up to hunt stag. As game theorists put the idea, because the situation in which we both hunt hare is less risky, given that we are uncertain about what the other player will do, hunting hare is the "risk-dominant" choice.

In analyzing games, the game theorist is looking for different situations of "equilibrium." As defined by mathematician John Nash, the players are in a situation of equilibrium when each adopts the best response he or she can, given that the other players are playing their best responses (where each decides according to specified preferences, e.g., for hunting stag over hunting hare, with a belief about what the other player will do). Given these motivations, no player has incentive to deviate from a situation of equilibrium—unless there is some change in what others are choosing. As long as no perturbation or shock interrupts the system, there is something of a stable balance, much as a large object (e.g., a plank or the Eiffel Tower) might sit at rest upon a fulcrum, with each of its sides balancing the other. (A gust of wind, a "shock" to the system, would throw the situation into disequilibrium or shift it to a new balance point.)

Now notice that a situation of social equilibrium needn't involve cooperation. In the stag hunt game, there are two situations of equilibrium, a cooperative equilibrium (both players hunt stag) and a noncooperative equilibrium (both players hunt hare). Each does best for him- or herself in hunting stag if others also cooperate. But, if everyone else goes it alone, each does best for him- or herself in hunting hare. There are two ways of doing as well as one can for oneself, given the choices of others, even as the players will do the very best if cooperation is established. If the cooperative equilibrium is not already established, the challenge is to get it started, by giving all parties enough assurance that others will be cooperating, so that all can move to a cooperative footing. If the cooperative equilibrium is already established, the challenge is to keep up assurances that others are still cooperating, so that the cooperative equilibrium doesn't collapse into the noncooperative equilibrium.

As an example of a real-life shift from a cooperative equilibrium to a worse, noncooperative one, think of a bank run or financial crisis that results from a sudden lack of "confidence." As long as all are keeping their money invested (by keeping one's savings with a bank or by otherwise lending or investing one's capital), all are better off under this situation of "cooperation." But if others aren't staying invested, if others aren't cooperating, each will do best not to be invested. Both are equilibrium situations. But whether the group stays in the cooperative equilibrium depends on how confident each is that others are also cooperating. When the level of confidence suddenly drops, because of a shock to the system (e.g., investment suddenly becomes less appealing, and each starts betting that the others will hold their funds instead), the group will move to a new equilibrium of noncooperation.

This, with a few further complications, is similar to how we imagine decline in a system of asshole capitalism. To see how this might work more precisely, consider a party. At the party, most people are unhip, but no one really minds, as long as there is plenty of beer. The beer will keep flowing only if it is regularly replenished by hourly beer runs. These require that each partygoer chip in with a modest contribution for each run. People like a good party, and they are happy to contribute, but their preference is conditional: in order for it to be worthwhile for them to contribute, most of the partygoers must also be contributing toward the cost of beer. So if the beer fund falls below a critical threshold, no one will be willing to contribute any longer. The fun will be over. (As people become sober, the party won't be enjoyable with so many unhip people.)

Let us imagine that the party starts off swimmingly. Everyone is having a fine time and regularly paying for beer. Everyone cooperates by making the contribution necessary for all to enjoy themselves. The situation is a cooperative equilibrium, meaning that the contribution is the best response for each, given that enough others are likewise contributing. As long as the situation doesn't change, the party will last.

But now imagine a shock to the system: new people arrive. These people are hip, so hip, in fact, that they don't feel they have to make a contribution. Their very presence, they assume, is contribution enough. Since the hipsters don't contribute, other partygoers feel as if they shouldn't have to contribute either. As the party wears on, fewer and fewer people contribute money for beer until the cooperative party is over. Everyone is worse off as the beerless, noncontributive equilibrium takes over.

We can model asshole capitalist decline in more or less the same way. As above, people start out willing to fully cooperate in the institutions and practices needed for capitalism to fulfill its social promises. This is a cooperative equilibrium. People will continue to cooperate as long as others are doing likewise. We then imagine a shock, a shift to an entitlement culture, which adds assholes to the system. The entitlement culture introduces incentives for assholery, by sending a message that gives moral license to reaping more of the benefits of cooperation and incurring less of its costs. When assholes become sufficiently numerous, cooperative people become unwilling to continue upholding supportive practices and institutions, leaving capitalism increasingly unable to deliver the goods. In time, this noncooperative relationship becomes the new equilibrium situation, to everyone's detriment.

The question for the formal theory of games then is how to formalize that idea. What is needed is a careful characterization of the preferences of the different players. Carvalho's suggestion is that one can do that in the following way. Suppose that a person's payoff from cooperating is:

$$xp - c$$

where p is the proportion of people he or she expects to cooperate, c is the cost of cooperating, and x is a positive constant. The positive constant places weight upon the proportion of cooperators in order to reflect the value that each player assigns to the cooperation of others.[1] Now normalize the payoff from not cooperating to zero. The person cooperates when:

$$xp - c > 0$$

or equivalently when:

$$p > cx$$

Further, we can conceive of a sense of duty to cooperate as a benefit or negative cost $c < 0$. (The same goes with the preference for a party with plenty of beer. Even if a person doesn't want any beer that hour, she still may feel a duty to pitch in.) Each player/partygoer sees moral reason to cooperate for its own sake. In this model, cooperation is a "dominant" strategy (i.e., each player is strictly better off following that strategy than following the other strategy). An agent cooperates regardless of

---

1. We thus adjust the value of x according to how we think the players will value the cooperation of others in the kind of situation in question. So if we want the cooperation of others to play a big role in the decision whether to cooperate, we let x equal something very large. Likewise, if we want the proportion of cooperators to count for less in the decision, i.e., if we want c to be more important than p, then x would have a smaller value.

Many plausible scenarios will balance these values. Consider what happens if we dramatically reduce the value of x, so that each player is relatively unaffected by the cooperation of others. In that kind of case, even a small increase in costs can mean that people won't cooperate. Or, more concretely, suppose $c = 1$, $x = 1$, and $p = 80$ percent. Then $xp - c = .80 - 1.00 = -.20$. Since this is less than zero, no one will cooperate. But this seems implausible in many cases, as when costs are in any case low and tons of people are cooperating. In that situation, people are often willing to cooperate as well. We better represent that situation, then, by instead, say, letting $x = 10$. Then $xp - c = 79$, which means that cooperation has an attractive payoff.

how many others cooperate—that is, for all p. If there's no cost to cooperation, because $c < 0$ for all agents, then universal cooperation is the only (Nash) equilibrium (i.e., cooperation is the best response, given that others are cooperating).

This system is stable as long as it is not interrupted. But now we imagine a shock, in which noncooperators—assholes (or hip people)—are introduced. The players' experience of what the assholes are choosing crowds out their moral motivations. The sense of duty is replaced by a sense of entitlement to do less than what cooperation requires. Thus c, the cost of cooperation, starts to rise. When expectations are "anchored" in or informed by the earlier cooperative equilibrium, cooperation will still be maintained for some time. But once the costs are high enough—say, when c exceeds $x/2$—the equilibrium in which no agent cooperates becomes risk dominant. As evolutionary models would put the point, "mutants" with uncooperative strategies will be able to invade the population and drive society toward an uncooperative equilibrium.

That is the main idea. We might also offer two further comments that suggest why this is of interest. First, notice that the situation is not the traditional "free-rider problem," in which noncooperators hobble cooperation by taking its benefits without bearing its costs out of *amoral, optimizing self-interest*. We have assumed the preferences of both cooperators and noncooperators alike are moralized. The asshole is motivated by his sense of *entitlement*. So the problem of asshole capitalist decline isn't a problem of amoral selfishness; it is a question of moral values.

Second, note that decline to noncooperation is not irreversible, at least in principle. While cooperation will decay for some time, there is room for hope that cooperation will return. It could be that the cost of cooperation falls, say, because the overall benefit of cooperation increases. In that case we'd expect that a cooperative cycle would eventually recommence, shifting us back to a cooperative equilibrium.

This is reason for hope, but also reason for eternal cooperative vigilance. For if we assume that "mutant" assholes also enter at later stages, there could be cycling between cooperative and noncooperative equilibriums, with periodic influence by assholes, in the mathematical limit. The work of asshole management, in short, is never finished.

AARON JAMES holds a PhD from Harvard and is associate professor of philosophy at the University of California, Irvine. He is the author of *Fairness in Practice: A Social Contract for a Global Economy* (New York: Oxford University Press, 2012) and numerous academic articles. He was awarded a Burkhardt fellowship from the American Council of Learned Societies, and spent the 2009–10 academic year at the Center for Advanced Study in the Behavioral Sciences at Stanford University. He's an avid surfer (the experience of which has directly inspired his theory of the asshole) . . . and he's not an asshole.

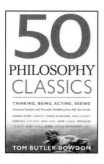

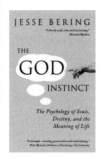